Advanced Microsoft Copilot Prompt Engi

A Step-by-Step Guide

Table of Content

I. Introduction

- Overview of Microsoft Copilot and its role in AI-assisted productivity.
- Importance of prompt engineering for maximizing efficiency and accuracy.
- Who this guide is for: developers, content creators, business professionals, etc.

II. Understanding Copilot's AI Mechanism

- How Microsoft Copilot processes and interprets prompts.
- Differences between Copilot in Microsoft 365, GitHub Copilot, and other versions.
- Limitations and strengths of Copilot's AI model.

III. Fundamentals of Prompt Engineering

- Key principles of effective prompts (clarity, context, specificity).
- Structuring prompts for optimal responses.
- The role of tone and language in AI comprehension.

IV. Step-by-Step Guide to Writing Advanced Prompts

Step 1: Defining Clear Objectives

- Understanding the goal of your prompt.
- Aligning prompts with specific tasks (coding, writing, data analysis, etc.).

Step 2: Providing Context and Constraints

- Including background information to refine responses.
- Using constraints such as word limits, styles, or formats.
- Examples of contextualized vs. non-contextualized prompts.

Step 3: Structuring Complex Prompts

- Breaking down multi-step requests.
- Using sequential prompts for detailed outputs.

- Leveraging bullet points, numbered lists, and keyword emphasis.

Step 4: Refining and Iterating Prompts

- Analyzing initial responses for improvement.
- Adjusting wording, specificity, and scope.
- Using feedback loops to enhance results.

Step 5: Leveraging Copilot for Specific Use Cases

- **For Coding**: Writing effective prompts for GitHub Copilot.
- **For Business Documents**: Crafting prompts for emails, reports, and presentations.
- **For Content Creation**: Generating blogs, marketing copy, and creative writing.

V. Common Pitfalls and How to Avoid Them

- Overly vague or ambiguous prompts.
- Providing conflicting instructions.
- Expecting Copilot to generate perfect responses without iteration.

VI. Advanced Techniques for Power Users

- Using chain-of-thought prompting for complex reasoning.
- Applying role-based prompting (e.g., "Act as a software engineer...").
- Fine-tuning prompts for industry-specific needs.

VII. Case Studies and Real-World Applications

- Examples of effective prompt engineering in different industries.
- Success stories of businesses leveraging Copilot efficiently.

VIII. Conclusion and Next Steps

- Recap of key strategies.
- Encouragement to experiment and refine prompts.
- Additional resources for deepening Copilot expertise

Foreword

We are living in an era where artificial intelligence is no longer a futuristic concept—it is a **present-day reality** that is reshaping the way we work, think, and create. **Microsoft Copilot** stands at the forefront of this transformation, empowering professionals across industries with AI-assisted capabilities that enhance productivity, streamline workflows, and unlock new creative possibilities.

Yet, as powerful as Copilot is, its effectiveness depends largely on **how well we communicate with it**. AI is not magic—it responds to the clarity, precision, and structure of the instructions we provide. This is where **prompt engineering** becomes essential. Understanding how to craft the right prompts can mean the difference between generic outputs and truly **insightful, tailored, and high-value responses**.

That is what makes this book so important. **"Advanced Microsoft Copilot Prompt Engineering – A Step-by-Step Guide"** is more than just a manual—it is a roadmap for anyone looking to harness **Copilot's full potential**. Whether you're a developer writing code, a business professional drafting reports, or a content creator generating ideas, this book provides you with **the strategies, techniques, and real-world applications** necessary to elevate your AI interactions.

I encourage you to not only read this book but to **experiment, refine, and iterate** on the principles it teaches. The future of AI-driven productivity is here, and by mastering prompt engineering, you are positioning yourself at the cutting edge of this revolution.

Welcome to the future of work. Let's make the most of it.

Donald Mwase
IT Enthusiast
February, 21 2025

Preface

Artificial intelligence is transforming the way we work, create, and solve problems. At the heart of this revolution is **Microsoft Copilot**, an AI-powered assistant designed to enhance productivity across coding, business documentation, content creation, and beyond. However, like any powerful tool, the key to unlocking its full potential lies in knowing how to use it effectively.

This book, **"Advanced Microsoft Copilot Prompt Engineering – A Step-by-Step Guide,"** is designed to help users go beyond basic commands and develop a **deep understanding of prompt engineering**. Whether you're a developer using GitHub Copilot, a business professional leveraging Copilot in Microsoft 365, or a content creator streamlining your workflow, mastering prompt engineering will allow you to achieve **greater accuracy, efficiency, and innovation**.

In the following chapters, you'll learn:

☑ **How Copilot processes and interprets prompts** to generate high-quality responses.

☑ **Key principles for crafting effective prompts**, including structure, tone, and clarity.

☑ **Advanced techniques** such as chain-of-thought prompting, role-based prompting, and contextualized inputs.

☑ **Common pitfalls to avoid**, ensuring that your prompts lead to **precise and actionable results**.

☑ **Real-world examples** across different industries, demonstrating how Copilot can be optimized for various tasks.

This guide is not just about using Copilot—it's about mastering **the art and science of communicating with AI**. By the end of this book, you'll have the skills to fine-tune your prompts, analyze responses for improvement, and develop a workflow that maximizes AI's potential.

AI is only as powerful as the instructions it receives. The better your prompts, the better your results. Let's embark on this journey to unlock the full power of Microsoft Copilot.

Happy prompting!

I. Introduction

Overview of Microsoft Copilot and Its Role in AI-Assisted Productivity

Microsoft Copilot is an advanced AI-powered assistant designed to enhance productivity across various domains, including business, software development, and content creation. Integrated seamlessly into Microsoft 365, GitHub, and other Microsoft services, Copilot leverages cutting-edge artificial intelligence models to automate tasks, streamline workflows, and provide intelligent recommendations. By understanding natural language prompts, Copilot enables users to work more efficiently, reducing the time spent on repetitive or complex activities.

One of Copilot's key strengths lies in its ability to enhance productivity within Microsoft 365 applications, such as Word, Excel, Outlook, and PowerPoint. In Word, it assists users by generating, summarizing, and refining text, making content creation faster and more effective. Excel users benefit from Copilot's ability to analyze data, create complex formulas, and generate visualizations, allowing for better decision-making with minimal effort. In Outlook, Copilot helps draft emails, summarize lengthy threads, and suggest responses, improving communication efficiency. Similarly, in PowerPoint, it generates slide decks based on user prompts, saving time on design and content structuring.

For developers, GitHub Copilot is a game-changer, acting as an AI-powered coding assistant that suggests code snippets, auto-completes functions, and even writes entire scripts based on user inputs. By understanding the context of the code, Copilot reduces the time spent searching for solutions and debugging, ultimately accelerating the development process. It supports multiple programming languages and integrates directly into popular development environments such as Visual Studio Code. This allows developers to focus more on problem-solving and innovation rather than routine coding tasks.

Beyond individual applications, Microsoft Copilot plays a crucial role in enterprise productivity by facilitating workflow automation and knowledge management. It helps businesses optimize processes by automating document generation, summarizing reports, and extracting insights from large datasets. Additionally, Copilot's AI-driven recommendations improve collaboration by providing contextual insights and intelligent suggestions within Microsoft Teams, enabling teams to work more effectively and make informed decisions faster.

Copilot's impact on AI-assisted productivity extends beyond traditional office tasks and development work. It enables professionals across industries—including marketing, finance, healthcare, and education—to enhance efficiency and innovation. Marketers use Copilot to draft compelling ad copy and generate campaign strategies, while financial analysts leverage it to interpret financial data and predict trends. In education, Copilot helps students and teachers by generating lesson plans, summarizing textbooks, and assisting with research.

As AI continues to evolve, Microsoft Copilot is expected to become even more powerful, integrating deeper into daily workflows and expanding its capabilities. By leveraging large language models and user-specific data, Copilot continuously learns and adapts to provide more relevant and accurate assistance. Whether streamlining business operations, improving coding efficiency, or enhancing communication, Microsoft Copilot is shaping the future of AI-assisted productivity by making complex tasks more manageable and empowering users to focus on high-value work.

The Importance of Prompt Engineering for Maximizing Efficiency and Accuracy

Prompt engineering plays a crucial role in optimizing the performance of AI-powered tools like Microsoft Copilot, ensuring users receive accurate, relevant, and high-quality responses. As AI models rely on natural language inputs to generate results, the way a prompt is structured directly affects the output. Well-crafted prompts can lead to precise and insightful answers, while vague or poorly structured prompts may produce irrelevant or misleading results. By mastering prompt engineering, users can significantly enhance their efficiency and maximize the value they get from AI assistance.

One of the key benefits of prompt engineering is improved **accuracy** in AI-generated responses. When users provide clear, specific, and well-defined prompts, AI tools like Copilot can better understand the context and deliver more relevant answers. For example, instead of asking, *"Write an email,"* a more effective prompt would be, *"Draft a professional email to a client requesting an update on the project timeline."* The second prompt provides essential details, such as tone, recipient, and purpose, leading to a more useful output. Without this level of clarity, the AI might generate a generic response that requires additional editing, reducing productivity.

Efficiency is another major advantage of well-structured prompts. By refining input queries, users can minimize the need for multiple revisions and re-prompts. A well-engineered prompt ensures that Copilot generates content that is as close as possible to the user's desired outcome, saving time and effort. In business settings, this can mean drafting emails faster, generating reports with accurate data insights, or creating well-structured presentations without unnecessary iterations. For developers, writing precise coding prompts can help Copilot generate functional code snippets without extensive debugging or manual corrections.

Prompt engineering also enhances **AI adaptability**, allowing users to guide the AI in a more controlled and intentional manner. AI models, including Copilot, operate based on probabilities and learned patterns rather than true comprehension. By incorporating context, constraints, and formatting instructions into prompts, users can influence how the AI processes information. For example, asking *"Summarize this report in bullet points under 100 words"* directs the AI to generate a concise and structured response, whereas a vague request like *"Summarize this"* may result in an overly detailed or disorganized output.

Moreover, effective prompt engineering reduces **misinterpretations and biases** in AI responses. Poorly framed prompts can lead to unintended outputs, introducing errors that require additional verification and edits. For example, if a prompt lacks specificity in a financial report generation task, the AI may assume incorrect timeframes or data parameters. Users who understand how to structure their queries properly can mitigate such risks, ensuring that AI-generated content aligns with their expectations and needs.

In technical applications, such as software development, prompt engineering helps **enhance AI-assisted coding** by improving Copilot's suggestions. Developers who specify programming languages, frameworks, and expected functionalities in their prompts receive more accurate and usable code snippets. For instance, instead of asking *"Generate a login function,"* specifying *"Generate a Python function using Flask for user authentication with JWT tokens"* yields a more relevant output. This level of precision allows developers to integrate AI-generated code directly into their projects with minimal adjustments, increasing workflow efficiency.

Beyond individual productivity, prompt engineering plays a vital role in enterprise AI integration, where AI models assist in automating business processes, decision-making, and customer interactions. Companies that train employees on prompt optimization can leverage AI to streamline operations, improve customer service, and generate high-quality business insights. By equipping teams with prompt engineering best practices, organizations can maximize the return on their AI investments while maintaining accuracy and efficiency in automated tasks.

As AI models continue to evolve, mastering prompt engineering will become an essential skill for professionals across industries. Whether used for writing, coding, data analysis, or business automation, effective prompt design ensures that AI tools like Microsoft Copilot function as intelligent and reliable assistants. By focusing on clarity, specificity, and structured inputs, users can harness the full power of AI-driven productivity while minimizing errors and inefficiencies.

Who This Guide Is For

This guide is designed for a wide range of professionals and individuals looking to harness the power of **Microsoft Copilot** through effective prompt engineering. Whether you are a business professional aiming to streamline daily tasks, a developer seeking efficient coding assistance, or a content creator looking to enhance your writing, understanding how to craft precise prompts will help you maximize Copilot's capabilities. By tailoring this guide to different user needs, we ensure that anyone leveraging AI for productivity gains valuable insights into prompt optimization.

Business Professionals and Corporate Users

For business professionals, Microsoft Copilot serves as a powerful assistant within **Microsoft 365 applications**, helping automate tasks like drafting emails, summarizing reports, generating presentations, and analyzing data in Excel. This guide will benefit executives, managers, sales teams, and administrative staff who rely on AI-powered tools to enhance communication and decision-making. By mastering prompt engineering, business users can ensure Copilot generates highly relevant and contextually accurate responses, saving time and improving efficiency in day-to-day operations.

Developers and Software Engineers

GitHub Copilot is revolutionizing the way developers write code by providing **real-time code suggestions, auto-completions, and debugging assistance**. This guide is particularly valuable for software engineers, data scientists, and IT professionals who want to refine their prompt-writing skills to get more precise and efficient code outputs. Whether you're working with Python, JavaScript, C++, or any other programming language, learning how to structure prompts properly can reduce errors, improve code readability, and accelerate development workflows.

Content Creators and Writers

For content creators, marketers, and writers, Microsoft Copilot can **generate blogs, marketing copy, social media content, and creative writing** with remarkable efficiency. However, the quality of AI-generated content depends heavily on the way prompts are structured. This guide will help writers craft detailed and specific prompts to produce well-organized, engaging, and polished content. Whether you are a journalist, copywriter, or social media strategist, learning to fine-tune prompts will enable you to maintain consistency and originality in AI-assisted writing.

Students and Educators

Students and educators can also benefit significantly from Microsoft Copilot by using it for **research, summarization, lesson planning, and academic writing**. For students, learning how to phrase queries effectively can help generate more accurate study materials, explanations, and summaries of complex topics. Educators, on the other hand, can use Copilot to create lesson plans, quizzes, and structured content for teaching. This guide will help both groups refine their prompts to get educational content that aligns with academic standards.

Data Analysts and Finance Professionals

For those working in data analysis, finance, or market research, Microsoft Copilot can assist in **data visualization, trend analysis, and financial reporting**. However, asking Copilot the right questions is crucial to obtaining meaningful insights. This guide will teach finance and data professionals how to write precise prompts that yield well-structured, insightful responses, enabling them to make informed decisions and present data in a more actionable format.

Customer Support and HR Teams

Customer service representatives and HR professionals can leverage Copilot for **automating responses, creating policy documents, and managing communication workflows**. Effective prompt engineering ensures that AI-generated responses are both accurate and aligned with company policies. This guide will show HR teams how to refine prompts for writing job descriptions, performance reviews, and employee communications while helping customer support teams craft AI-assisted responses that improve customer satisfaction.

Why This Guide Matters for All Users

Regardless of your profession or industry, mastering prompt engineering is key to unlocking the full potential of Microsoft Copilot. AI tools are only as effective as the instructions they receive, and a well-structured prompt can mean the difference between an unhelpful response and a highly efficient AI-assisted task. This guide is designed to help users across different fields understand how to **communicate with AI more effectively, reduce errors, and optimize their workflows**, ensuring that Copilot serves as a truly valuable productivity partner.

By the end of this guide, users will be equipped with practical strategies and best practices for writing clear, structured, and goal-oriented prompts. Whether you are automating business processes, coding complex applications, or generating compelling content, learning the art of **prompt engineering** will enable you to **work smarter, faster, and more accurately with Microsoft Copilot**.

II. Understanding Copilot's AI Mechanism

How Microsoft Copilot Processes and Interprets Prompts

Microsoft Copilot operates using advanced artificial intelligence models that process and interpret user prompts through **natural language understanding (NLU)** and **context-driven machine learning**. When a user inputs a request, Copilot analyzes the structure, intent, and context of the prompt to generate a relevant and coherent response. The effectiveness of its response depends on how well the prompt is formulated, as the AI relies on pattern recognition, pre-trained data, and user-provided context to produce accurate results.

At the core of Copilot's processing mechanism is **large language model (LLM) technology**, which enables it to understand human-like language, predict responses, and generate meaningful content. These models have been trained on vast datasets, including publicly available text, structured data, and programming code, allowing Copilot to provide intelligent suggestions in various domains. When a user submits a query, Copilot first breaks it down into **key components**—identifying the main request, relevant context, and any constraints specified. For example, a prompt like *"Summarize* *this document in three bullet points"* signals that the AI should extract the most critical information while adhering to a structured format.

One of the most important aspects of how Copilot interprets prompts is its **ability to use context**. Context can come from multiple sources, such as previous prompts in an ongoing conversation, user-specified parameters, or even the application in which Copilot is being used. For example, in **Microsoft Word**, Copilot can analyze an entire document and generate content that aligns with its existing tone and structure. In **Excel**, it processes spreadsheet data to suggest formulas, analyze trends, and provide visualizations. Similarly, in **GitHub Copilot**, it understands programming context by examining surrounding code, variable names, and function definitions to offer accurate code suggestions.

Another critical aspect of Copilot's interpretation process is its **use of probabilistic reasoning**. Instead of "understanding" a prompt in a human sense, the AI predicts the most likely and relevant response based on patterns it has learned. It ranks potential responses and generates the most appropriate output based on probability. This means that slight variations in how a prompt is worded can lead to different responses. For instance, asking *"Write a Python function for data sorting"* might yield a generic sorting algorithm, whereas specifying *"Write a Python function to sort a list of integers using quicksort"* will prompt Copilot to generate a more targeted and optimized solution.

Moreover, Copilot continuously refines its responses by incorporating **user feedback and iterative learning**. If a user rephrases a prompt or provides additional context, Copilot adjusts its interpretation to align more closely with the user's intent. This iterative approach allows users to fine-tune their interactions with Copilot, making it a more powerful and responsive tool.

However, Copilot also has **limitations** in processing and interpreting prompts. Because it does not possess actual comprehension or reasoning abilities, it may sometimes misinterpret vague or ambiguous requests. For example, if a user asks, *"Generate a report,"* without specifying the topic, format, or key points, Copilot might produce a generic or incorrect response. Additionally, since it relies on pre-trained data and user input, it may not always produce the most up-to-date or domain-specific information unless explicitly guided through a well-structured prompt.

To optimize Copilot's performance, users should provide **clear, detailed, and structured prompts** that include necessary context and constraints. This ensures that Copilot generates responses that are both relevant and useful, minimizing the need for extensive revisions. By understanding how Copilot processes and interprets prompts, users can craft better queries and unlock the full potential of AI-assisted productivity.

Differences Between Copilot in Microsoft 365, GitHub Copilot, and Other Versions

Microsoft Copilot comes in multiple versions, each tailored to specific use cases and applications. The most well-known variants include **Copilot in Microsoft 365**, which focuses on business productivity, and **GitHub Copilot**, which serves as an AI-powered coding assistant. Additionally, Microsoft has extended Copilot's capabilities to other platforms, such as Windows, Edge, and Azure, each with distinct features. While all these versions leverage large language models (LLMs) to enhance user efficiency, they differ in their integration, purpose, and functionality.

Copilot in Microsoft 365: AI for Business Productivity

Microsoft 365 Copilot is designed to enhance workplace productivity by integrating AI-powered assistance into applications like **Word, Excel, Outlook, PowerPoint, and Teams**. This version of Copilot acts as a digital assistant that helps professionals streamline tasks such as drafting documents, analyzing data, summarizing emails, and generating presentations.

In **Word**, Copilot assists users by generating text, rewriting content, and suggesting improvements based on the document's tone and style. In **Excel**, it helps analyze complex datasets by suggesting formulas, creating pivot tables, and generating charts with minimal user input. **PowerPoint users** benefit from Copilot's ability to convert text-based outlines into visually engaging slides. Meanwhile, in **Outlook**, Copilot improves email management by drafting responses, summarizing long email threads, and organizing schedules. In **Microsoft Teams**, Copilot enhances collaboration by summarizing meetings, generating discussion points, and offering action items.

Unlike other versions, Microsoft 365 Copilot is primarily focused on **business automation and document generation**, helping professionals save time on routine office tasks. It is deeply integrated into the Microsoft ecosystem and is best suited for corporate environments where efficiency, data-driven insights, and seamless collaboration are essential.

GitHub Copilot: AI-Powered Coding Assistant

GitHub Copilot, developed in partnership with OpenAI, is specifically designed for **software development**. It integrates into **Visual Studio Code, JetBrains, and other development environments** to assist programmers by **suggesting code snippets, auto-completing functions, and even writing entire blocks of code**.

This version of Copilot works by analyzing the surrounding code context and predicting what the developer intends to write next. For example, if a programmer starts writing a function definition in Python, GitHub Copilot can suggest the full implementation based on best practices and learned patterns from public repositories. It supports multiple programming languages, including Python, JavaScript, C++, Java, and Go, making it versatile for developers across different domains.

One of GitHub Copilot's key strengths is its ability to **understand programming logic, syntax, and frameworks**. Unlike Microsoft 365 Copilot, which focuses on text and data manipulation, GitHub Copilot is built to enhance **code efficiency, reduce errors, and improve productivity in software development**. It is particularly useful for **automating repetitive coding tasks**, generating boilerplate code, and helping new programmers learn best practices through contextual suggestions.

However, **GitHub Copilot does not have deep integration with business applications** like Microsoft 365 Copilot. Instead, it is optimized for **developer workflows** and relies heavily on public code repositories, which means that the quality of suggestions can vary depending on the project and programming language used.

Other Versions of Microsoft Copilot

Beyond Microsoft 365 and GitHub Copilot, Microsoft has introduced Copilot into several other platforms to extend AI-driven assistance across different domains:

- **Windows Copilot:** This version is integrated directly into Windows 11, offering AI-powered assistance for navigating the OS, adjusting settings, summarizing text, and integrating with Microsoft Edge and Bing Chat. It acts as a **personalized assistant** for general users, helping with tasks such as file management, system troubleshooting, and browsing assistance.
- **Copilot in Edge & Bing Chat:** Microsoft has embedded Copilot into the **Edge browser and Bing search engine**, providing users with AI-driven web search enhancements, conversational answers, and summarization capabilities. This version is optimized for **research, content discovery, and quick information retrieval**, making it useful for students, researchers, and casual users looking for intelligent search assistance.
- **Azure OpenAI Copilot:** Designed for **enterprise AI applications**, this version allows businesses to integrate AI-powered automation into their workflows using Microsoft's cloud infrastructure. Organizations can customize Copilot to interact with proprietary databases, customer support systems, and knowledge bases, making it a powerful tool for large-scale automation and decision-making.

Key Differences in Purpose and Use Cases

While all versions of Copilot use AI to enhance productivity, they serve **different user needs** and environments:

Feature	Microsoft 365 Copilot	GitHub Copilot	Windows/Edge/Bing Copilot	Azure OpenAI Copilot
Primary Use	Business productivity (documents, emails, spreadsheets)	Software development (coding assistance)	General AI assistance (OS navigation, search, summarization)	Enterprise AI automation (custom workflows, business solutions)
Key Applications	Word, Excel, PowerPoint, Outlook, Teams	Visual Studio Code, JetBrains, GitHub	Windows 11, Edge Browser, Bing Search	Microsoft Azure, enterprise AI platforms
Integration	Deeply integrated with Microsoft 365 apps	Integrated into IDEs and coding environments	Integrated into Windows, Edge, and Bing	Cloud-based AI for business applications
Strengths	Automates office tasks, enhances collaboration, provides document insights	Generates and completes code, reduces development time, supports multiple languages	Assists with browsing, system commands, and search queries	Customizable AI for large-scale business automation
Best For	Business professionals, corporate teams	Developers, software engineers, IT professionals	General users, researchers, students	Enterprises, data analysts, AI-powered business solutions

Conclusion

Microsoft Copilot is a versatile AI tool, but its different versions serve distinct audiences. **Microsoft 365 Copilot** is designed for business professionals looking to automate office tasks, while **GitHub Copilot** is optimized for developers who need AI-powered coding assistance. Other versions, such as **Windows Copilot, Edge Copilot, and Azure OpenAI Copilot**, cater to broader AI applications, from **OS navigation and research** to **enterprise AI automation**. Understanding these differences allows users to choose the right version of Copilot based on their specific needs, ensuring they maximize efficiency and productivity in their respective domains.

Limitations and Strengths of Copilot's AI Model

Microsoft Copilot, powered by advanced large language models (LLMs) like OpenAI's GPT-4, is a groundbreaking AI assistant designed to enhance productivity across various applications. While Copilot offers **remarkable strengths** in assisting with tasks like writing, coding, and data analysis, it also has inherent **limitations** that users should be aware of. Understanding these strengths and weaknesses allows users to **maximize its potential while mitigating its shortcomings**.

Strengths of Copilot's AI Model

1. Enhances Productivity and Efficiency

One of Copilot's biggest strengths is its ability to **automate repetitive and time-consuming tasks**, significantly improving productivity. In **Microsoft 365 applications**, Copilot helps users draft emails, summarize lengthy documents, and generate data insights in Excel within seconds. In **GitHub Copilot**, it assists developers by suggesting code snippets, completing functions, and reducing manual coding efforts. These capabilities enable professionals to focus on higher-level strategic work rather than mundane tasks.

2. Context-Aware Assistance

Copilot is designed to **understand and adapt to user context** within its supported applications. For instance, in **Microsoft Word**, it considers document structure and tone before generating text, ensuring that content aligns with the user's writing style. Similarly, in **Excel**, Copilot analyzes existing data to provide relevant formulas and insights. In **GitHub Copilot**, it looks at surrounding code to generate intelligent suggestions that match coding conventions and best practices. This ability to adapt contextually makes Copilot a highly intuitive AI assistant.

3. Supports Multiple Domains and Industries

Copilot is versatile and **serves a wide range of users across different industries**. It is beneficial to business professionals, developers, students, educators, data analysts, and more. Whether used for **writing reports, generating marketing content, coding software, or analyzing financial trends**, Copilot provides tailored assistance that meets diverse professional needs. Its integration into Microsoft's ecosystem ensures that it can be leveraged across various fields, from corporate environments to software development.

4. Natural Language Understanding (NLU) and Ease of Use

Unlike traditional automation tools that require programming or scripting, Copilot uses **natural language processing (NLP) to understand human-like instructions**. This means that even users with no technical expertise can interact with it effectively by providing simple, structured prompts. This ease of use makes AI-driven productivity accessible to a broader audience, including those who are not familiar with complex software tools.

5. Continuous Improvement and AI Learning

Microsoft regularly updates Copilot with **enhanced AI models, improved prompt understanding, and refined responses**. Over time, as AI systems become more sophisticated, Copilot continues to improve its accuracy and contextual awareness. Users can also refine their interactions with Copilot by adjusting their prompts or providing feedback, allowing the AI to generate better responses.

Limitations of Copilot's AI Model

1. Dependence on Prompt Quality

One of Copilot's main weaknesses is that its **output quality heavily depends on the input prompt**. If a user provides a vague or poorly structured prompt, the AI may generate **inaccurate, incomplete, or irrelevant responses**. For example, asking *"Write an email"* without specifying the purpose, recipient, or tone may lead to a generic result that does not meet the user's needs. Users must refine their prompts by adding context, constraints, and specific instructions to achieve better results.

2. Limited Real-Time Knowledge and Data Freshness

While Copilot is trained on vast amounts of publicly available data, it **does not have real-time access to the internet or the latest information** unless explicitly connected to a live data source (such as Bing search for certain queries). This means it may provide outdated or incomplete information, especially when dealing with **rapidly changing fields like finance, technology, or current events**. Users should verify AI-generated content before relying on it for critical decision-making.

3. Potential for Bias and Inaccuracies

Like all AI models, Copilot is trained on large datasets that may contain **inherent biases**. This can sometimes result in **biased, misleading, or inappropriate responses**, particularly in sensitive topics like politics, ethics, or legal matters. Additionally, because the AI **does not "understand" information the way humans do**, it may generate responses that sound plausible but contain factual inaccuracies (also known as AI "hallucinations"). Users should always **fact-check and critically evaluate** Copilot's responses before using them in important contexts.

4. Inability to Handle Complex Reasoning and Creativity at a Human Level

While Copilot excels at automating tasks and generating content based on patterns, it **cannot perform deep reasoning, critical thinking, or truly creative problem-solving at a human level**. For example, it can summarize a business report or suggest code, but it cannot **strategically plan a company's future** or **develop innovative scientific theories**. Users should treat Copilot as a **support tool rather than a replacement for human expertise**.

5. Privacy and Security Considerations

Since Copilot processes user data to generate responses, there are potential **privacy and security risks**, especially in corporate and sensitive environments. Microsoft has implemented strict security measures for Copilot in **enterprise applications**, ensuring that AI-generated content complies with data protection policies. However, users must still exercise caution when using AI for **confidential business operations, personal data, or proprietary code**. Organizations should establish clear guidelines on **what types of data can be safely shared with AI tools**.

6. Limited Customization and Adaptability Outside Its Predefined Scope

While Copilot is highly useful within its designated applications (Microsoft 365, GitHub, Windows, etc.), it **struggles with tasks that fall outside its training scope**. Unlike enterprise AI models that can be fine-tuned for specific use cases (such as custom AI models built in Azure), Copilot is a **general-purpose AI assistant** that may not be suitable for highly specialized industries like advanced scientific research, legal analysis, or medical diagnosis.

Balancing Copilot's Strengths and Limitations

To make the most of Copilot's strengths while mitigating its weaknesses, users should:

- **Craft well-structured and detailed prompts** to ensure more accurate responses.
- **Verify information generated by Copilot**, especially when using it for research, business decisions, or financial analysis.
- **Use Copilot as a productivity tool rather than a replacement for human expertise**—leveraging its assistance while applying critical thinking.
- **Be mindful of privacy and security concerns**, especially when working with sensitive or proprietary data.
- **Stay updated on AI advancements**, as Copilot's capabilities continue to improve with Microsoft's ongoing updates.

By understanding both the **capabilities and limitations of Copilot**, users can optimize their workflows and enhance their efficiency without over-relying on AI for critical decision-making. Copilot is a powerful tool, but like any AI system, it works best **when used thoughtfully and strategically**.

III. Fundamentals of Prompt Engineering

Key Principles of Effective Prompts

Prompt engineering is a critical skill for maximizing the effectiveness of AI tools like **Microsoft Copilot**. A well-crafted prompt can significantly enhance the accuracy, relevance, and usefulness of AI-generated responses. The key to success lies in understanding **how AI models interpret language** and structuring prompts in a way that provides clear instructions, sufficient context, and well-defined constraints. Below are the fundamental principles of effective prompts that can help users generate high-quality responses from Copilot.

1. Clarity and Specificity

One of the most important principles of effective prompt design is **clarity**. A vague or ambiguous prompt can lead to **incomplete, irrelevant, or overly generic responses**. To improve accuracy, prompts should be **specific, detailed, and free from unnecessary complexity**.

For example, a prompt like:
❌ *"Write about artificial intelligence."*
is too broad and can result in a general, unfocused response.

Instead, a clearer and more specific prompt would be:
✅ *"Write a 200-word summary explaining how artificial intelligence is used in healthcare, including examples of AI applications in diagnostics and treatment."*

By adding details such as **word count, topic focus, and examples**, the AI can generate a more relevant and precise response.

2. Provide Context

AI models like Copilot do not inherently understand **background knowledge or user intent** unless explicitly provided in the prompt. Adding relevant **context** helps the AI produce responses that align with user expectations.

For instance, if asking Copilot to generate content for a business proposal, consider including:

- **Industry details** (e.g., healthcare, finance, technology)
- **Target audience** (e.g., investors, executives, customers)
- **Tone/style** (e.g., formal, persuasive, data-driven)

Example:

☑ *"Generate a one-page executive summary for a business proposal introducing a telemedicine startup. The audience is potential investors, and the tone should be formal and persuasive."*

By setting the context clearly, Copilot can tailor its response to **match the user's needs more effectively**.

3. Use Step-by-Step Instructions

Breaking down a request into **clear, sequential steps** helps AI understand complex prompts better. Instead of issuing a single vague command, provide a **structured sequence of instructions**.

For example:

✗ *"Analyze this dataset and give insights."*
☑ *"Analyze this dataset by identifying key trends, summarizing the top three insights, and suggesting one potential business strategy based on the findings."*

This approach **guides the AI through multiple steps**, ensuring a well-organized response that addresses different aspects of the request.

4. Define Constraints and Output Format

Copilot's responses can vary widely depending on the prompt's structure. Users can **control the output format** by specifying constraints such as **word limit, tone, response structure, or data format**.

Examples:

☑ *"Summarize this report in three bullet points, each under 20 words."*

☑ *"Write a persuasive email in a professional tone, no longer than 150 words."*
☑ *"Generate Python code for sorting a list of numbers using the quicksort algorithm, with inline comments explaining each step."*

By providing constraints, users can **prevent excessive, disorganized, or off-topic responses**.

5. Use Examples to Guide the AI

Providing **examples** within a prompt can significantly improve the **relevance and quality** of the AI's response. Examples help Copilot **understand the expected style, structure, and depth** of the output.

For instance, if requesting Copilot to write a job description:
☑ *"Write a job description for a Data Analyst role. Use the following format:*

1. **Job Title**
2. **Responsibilities**
3. **Required Skills**
4. **Preferred Qualifications**

Example:
'Software Engineer - Responsibilities: Develop scalable applications... Required Skills: Python, SQL...'"

Including a format or sample text allows Copilot to **mirror the desired structure** in its response.

6. Experiment and Iterate for Optimization

AI models do not always generate the perfect response on the first attempt. Users should **experiment with different wording, levels of detail, and formatting** to refine their prompts.

For instance, if the AI produces an **overly broad response**, try:

- Adding **more details** (*e.g., focus on one aspect of the topic*)
- Specifying a **response format** (*e.g., list, table, paragraph*)

- Adjusting the **tone and audience** (*e.g., formal, conversational*)

If an initial prompt doesn't yield the expected results, **reword it and try again**.

7. Consider the AI's Limitations

AI models **lack human intuition, deep reasoning, and up-to-date real-world knowledge**. Users should account for these limitations by:

- Avoiding prompts that require **real-time or factual updates** (*e.g., "What is the current stock price of Apple?"*)
- Not expecting **human-like creativity or emotional understanding** (*e.g., AI may struggle with highly nuanced creative writing or humor*)
- Fact-checking responses, especially for **critical business or research applications**

Example:
Instead of asking:
✗ *"Explain the latest scientific discovery in quantum computing."*
Try:
☑ *"Summarize key advancements in quantum computing based on publicly available research as of 2023."*

This helps prevent the AI from **providing outdated or speculative responses**.

8. Keep Prompts Concise but Informative

While details improve accuracy, **overloading a prompt with excessive information** can confuse the AI and lead to inconsistent results. The key is to **balance conciseness with clarity**.

✗ *"Write a marketing email for a new fitness app that tracks workouts, provides diet plans, offers personalized coaching, syncs with wearable devices, integrates with social media, has AI-powered recommendations, and is compatible with Android and iOS. The email should be engaging, persuasive, and under 200 words."*

✅ *"Write a 150-200 word marketing email for a new fitness app. Focus on its ability to track workouts, provide personalized coaching, and sync with wearable devices. The tone should be engaging and persuasive."*

By keeping the prompt **focused**, the AI can generate a **well-structured and readable response**.

Conclusion

Mastering the art of prompt engineering is key to unlocking the full potential of Microsoft Copilot and other AI models. By applying principles like **clarity, context, step-by-step instructions, constraints, examples, and iteration**, users can significantly improve the accuracy and relevance of AI-generated responses. While Copilot is a powerful tool, it works best when given **clear, structured, and well-defined prompts** that guide it toward producing high-quality results. With practice and refinement, users can develop prompts that maximize **efficiency, accuracy, and AI-assisted productivity**.

Structuring Prompts for Optimal Responses

The way a prompt is structured plays a crucial role in the quality, accuracy, and relevance of the response generated by AI tools like **Microsoft Copilot**. A well-structured prompt can help guide the AI toward the desired output, ensuring that responses are **coherent, specific, and useful**. In contrast, poorly structured prompts can lead to vague, irrelevant, or incomplete responses. To maximize efficiency and effectiveness, users should follow key principles when structuring their prompts.

1. Start with a Clear and Direct Instruction

Every prompt should begin with a **clear and direct request** that immediately tells the AI what is needed. The more precise the instruction, the more relevant the output.

For example, instead of asking:
✗ *"Tell me about marketing."*

A better-structured prompt would be:
☑ *"Provide an overview of digital marketing, including key strategies, benefits, and common challenges."*

By clearly stating the **topic and expected details**, the AI can generate a response that aligns with user expectations.

2. Define the Scope and Context

AI tools **do not have built-in awareness of user intent or context** unless explicitly provided. To improve the relevance of responses, prompts should specify:

- **Topic focus** (e.g., SEO marketing vs. general marketing)
- **Target audience** (e.g., beginners, professionals, students)
- **Tone and style** (e.g., formal, conversational, persuasive)

Example:
☑ *"Explain the basics of SEO marketing to a beginner. Use simple language and provide real-world examples."*

By defining the **target audience** and expected **level of detail**, the response will be **more tailored and useful**.

3. Specify the Format of the Response

AI-generated content can vary significantly depending on how the prompt is structured. To ensure that the response is delivered in the most useful format, users should specify whether they want:

- **A paragraph summary**
- **A bulleted list**
- **A table comparison**
- **Step-by-step instructions**

Example:
☑ *"List five key benefits of remote work in bullet points."*

✅ *"Compare in a table the advantages and disadvantages of remote work vs. in-office work."*

By predefining the **structure of the response**, users can obtain **organized, readable, and actionable** information.

4. Use Step-by-Step Instructions for Complex Queries

For multi-step processes, coding assistance, or decision-making guidance, it is helpful to **break down the request into separate steps** to ensure a structured response.

For instance, instead of asking:
❌ *"How do I create a social media marketing plan?"*

A better prompt would be:
✅ *"Explain how to create a social media marketing plan in five steps. Each step should include key actions and best practices."*

This approach results in **clear, actionable guidance** rather than a generic response.

5. Provide Examples for Better Accuracy

Including examples within the prompt helps **guide the AI's understanding** of the expected output style, tone, or level of detail.

Example:
✅ *"Write a professional email requesting a meeting. Example: 'Dear [Name], I hope this email finds you well...'"*

By providing a sample or desired structure, Copilot can **mimic the example and generate a more refined response**.

6. Set Constraints to Control Output Length and Depth

If a response is too lengthy or too vague, users can **control its depth and length** by setting constraints, such as:

- **Word count limits** (e.g., "Summarize this in 100 words.")
- **Level of detail** (e.g., "Provide a high-level overview.")
- **Time constraints** (e.g., "List three key tech trends for 2024.")

Example:

☑ *"Summarize the main features of Microsoft Teams in 50 words or less."*

Constraints help prevent **excessively long or unfocused responses**.

7. Iterate and Refine for Better Results

Not every AI response will be perfect on the first try. Users should be prepared to:

1. **Analyze the output** – Is it relevant and accurate?
2. **Adjust the prompt** – Add missing details or change the wording.
3. **Test multiple variations** – Try different phrasing to compare responses.

For instance, if the AI provides an overly broad answer, users can refine the prompt by adding:

- **More specific instructions** (e.g., "Focus only on social media strategies.")
- **Additional context** (e.g., "Provide examples from small businesses.")
- **Alternative response format** (e.g., "Give a numbered list of key steps.")

This process ensures the AI delivers **more precise and useful results** over time.

Conclusion

Structuring prompts effectively is essential for maximizing the potential of **Microsoft Copilot** and other AI tools. By following principles such as **clear instructions, defined scope, response formatting, step-by-step guidance, constraints, and iteration**, users can generate **more accurate, relevant, and actionable responses**. Whether for writing, research, coding, or analysis, well-structured prompts **enhance productivity and efficiency**, ensuring that AI assists in the most meaningful way possible.

The Role of Tone and Language in AI Comprehension

Language and tone play a significant role in how AI systems like **Microsoft Copilot** process and generate responses. Since AI models rely on text-based inputs to interpret meaning, the way a prompt is phrased—including word choice, sentence structure, and emotional tone—can greatly impact the quality, accuracy, and relevance of the response. Understanding how language influences AI comprehension can help users craft better prompts and obtain more precise, contextually appropriate results.

1. How AI Interprets Language and Meaning

AI models are trained on vast datasets containing text from books, articles, websites, and other sources. However, unlike humans, AI does not have an inherent **understanding of meaning, emotions, or intent**. Instead, it relies on **patterns, probability, and context** to predict and generate responses.

For example, if given the prompt:
✅ *"Explain how artificial intelligence is transforming the healthcare industry."*

Copilot will recognize keywords like "artificial intelligence" and "healthcare industry" and generate a response based on **patterns from its training data**. However, if the language in the prompt is vague or ambiguous, the AI may struggle to provide a focused answer.

❌ *"Tell me something about AI."*

This prompt lacks specificity, leaving the AI to **guess** what the user wants—leading to a broad or generic response. Therefore, **precise language is essential for AI comprehension and accuracy**.

2. The Importance of Tone in AI Responses

Tone refers to the **emotional or stylistic quality** of language, such as formal, casual, professional, or conversational. While AI does not **feel emotions**, it can detect tone based on word choice and sentence structure. The tone of a prompt **influences the tone of the AI's response**.

For example:
✅ *"Write a formal email requesting a meeting with a client."* (Response will likely be professional and structured.)

✅ *"Write a friendly and engaging invitation for a company event."* (Response will be more casual and inviting.)

Setting the **tone explicitly** ensures that the AI generates content that aligns with the user's needs. If the prompt lacks tone direction, the AI may default to a neutral or overly generic style.

3. Formal vs. Informal Language in AI Prompts

The distinction between **formal and informal language** is crucial in AI-generated text. Users can adjust prompts to fit different contexts by modifying word choice and sentence structure.

Formal   **Prompt:**

☑ *"Draft a business proposal outlining the key objectives and benefits of our new product launch. Ensure the tone is professional and persuasive."*

Informal   **Prompt:**

☑ *"Write a fun and engaging social media post announcing our new product launch. Keep the tone light and friendly."*

These slight changes in wording help AI understand **how to frame its response** appropriately. Formal prompts tend to yield **structured, data-driven, and professional outputs**, whereas informal prompts lead to **more conversational and engaging responses**.

4. Using Neutral, Positive, and Negative Tones for Different Contexts

AI models can adjust their responses based on whether the input tone is **neutral, positive, or negative**. However, AI does not have personal opinions, so users must carefully guide its output.

Neutral   **Prompt:**

☑ *"Summarize the key features of Microsoft Teams."*
(Response will be objective and informative.)

Positive   **Prompt:**

☑ *"Highlight the top benefits of Microsoft Teams and explain why it improves workplace collaboration."*
(Response will focus on advantages and productivity.)

Negative   **Prompt:**

☑ *"Discuss some of the limitations of Microsoft Teams and potential challenges users may face."*
(Response will focus on drawbacks and concerns.)

By adjusting **tone direction**, users can obtain responses that align with specific perspectives or use cases.

5. The Role of Clear and Concise Language

AI models function best when given **clear, direct, and concise prompts**. Unnecessarily complex or overly wordy prompts can lead to **confusing or inconsistent responses**.

Less   Effective   Prompt:
❌ *"Could you maybe, if possible, give me some sort of general idea about how AI has been somewhat useful in the past few years?"*

More   Effective   Prompt:
✅ *"Summarize key advancements in AI over the past five years."*

The second prompt eliminates **unnecessary words**, making it easier for AI to **process and generate a precise response**.

6. Ambiguity and AI Misinterpretation

AI **struggles with ambiguous language** because it lacks human intuition. If a prompt is too vague or open-ended, the response may be **off-topic or incomplete**.

For   example:
❌   *"Tell   me   about   banks."*
(AI may not know whether the user is referring to **financial institutions or riverbanks**.)

✅   *"Explain   the   role   of   commercial   banks   in   the   global   economy."*
(This version removes ambiguity and ensures a focused response.)

When crafting prompts, it is essential to **use precise wording and clarify the intended meaning**.

7. Cultural and Linguistic Considerations

AI models are trained on diverse datasets, but they may not always understand **regional dialects, slang, or cultural nuances**. Users should be mindful of this when phrasing prompts.

For   example:

✖   *"Give   me   the   411   on   blockchain."*
("411" is slang for information, but AI may not always interpret it correctly.)

☑ *"Provide an overview of blockchain technology, including its key benefits and applications."*
(This version uses standard, globally understood language.)

When working with AI, **standardized, widely recognized language** leads to more reliable and accurate responses.

8. Adjusting Tone and Language for Different AI Applications

Different versions of **Microsoft Copilot** (e.g., Copilot in Microsoft 365 vs. GitHub Copilot) respond better to certain types of prompts. The **appropriate tone and language** depend on the AI's intended use:

- **Business Writing (Copilot in Microsoft 365)** → Requires **formal, structured** prompts.
- **Coding Assistance (GitHub Copilot)** → Requires **precise, technical** prompts.
- **Creative Writing (AI Chatbots)** → Can be more **open-ended and imaginative**.

Understanding the **AI's intended function** ensures that prompts are **optimized for the best results**.

Conclusion

Tone and language are **essential components of AI comprehension**. While AI models do not possess human emotions, they rely on **patterns in text** to interpret and generate responses. By using **clear, precise, and structured language**, and by specifying **tone, format, and context**, users can significantly improve the **accuracy, relevance, and effectiveness** of AI-generated content. Mastering the role of **tone and language in AI prompts** ensures that Microsoft Copilot and other AI tools become **powerful assets for productivity, creativity, and problem-solving**.

IV. Step-by-Step Guide to Writing Advanced Prompts

Step 1: Defining Clear Objectives

Understanding the Goal of Your Prompt and How to Craft Effective Inputs

One of the most crucial aspects of **Microsoft Copilot** and other AI-powered tools is ensuring that your prompts are designed with a clear goal in mind. The AI can generate a wide range of responses, from technical explanations and business reports to creative writing and coding assistance. However, the quality and usefulness of the output depend significantly on how well the **goal of the prompt** is defined. By understanding what you want to achieve before crafting your prompt, you can improve accuracy, efficiency, and relevance.

1. Identifying the Purpose of Your Prompt

Before entering a prompt, take a moment to determine what you are trying to achieve. Ask yourself:

- **Do I need factual information or an opinion-based response?**
- **Am I looking for a summary or an in-depth explanation?**
- **Should the response be formal, conversational, or persuasive?**
- **Do I need the information to be structured in a specific format (e.g., bullet points, numbered lists, paragraphs)?**

Clearly defining your objective ensures that Copilot provides the **most relevant** and **useful** response.

Example:

✗ *"Tell me about AI."* (Too vague—what aspect of AI?)

☑ *"Summarize the benefits of AI in healthcare with real-world examples."* (Clear goal: specific industry, benefits, and examples.)

2. Tailoring Prompts for Different Use Cases

Different types of tasks require different styles of prompting. Below are several **common use cases** along with examples of well-structured prompts that define a clear goal.

a) Informational Requests (Factual Data & Explanations)

If your goal is to **obtain factual information**, structure your prompt so that it guides the AI to generate **concise, accurate, and relevant** details.

Example:

☑ *"Explain the key differences between machine learning and deep learning in simple terms."*
(Goal: Educational explanation for non-experts.)

☑ *"List five major breakthroughs in artificial intelligence from the past decade."*
(Goal: Specific list of advancements.)

By adding **specific instructions** such as "in simple terms" or "list five," you refine the AI's focus and get **better results**.

b) Summarization & Condensation

Sometimes, you may need **a brief summary** rather than a detailed explanation. Being clear about the **length** and **scope** helps optimize the output.

Example:

☑ *"Summarize the key points of the Agile project management methodology in 100 words."*
(Goal: Concise overview with a word limit.)

☑ *"Provide a one-paragraph summary of the main themes in 'To Kill a Mockingbird'."*
(Goal: Short, focused summary.)

By specifying **length constraints**, Copilot avoids generating **overly long** or **insufficiently detailed** responses.

c) Step-by-Step Instructions

For processes and tutorials, **break down** the prompt to ensure the AI provides **logical, ordered steps**.

Example:
✅ *"Explain how to set up two-factor authentication in Microsoft 365 in five steps."*
(Goal: Clear, numbered steps for easy implementation.)

✅ *"Describe how to write a business plan, including key sections and best practices."*
(Goal: Comprehensive guide with structure.)

Using phrases like **"in five steps"** or **"including key sections"** helps structure the response logically.

d) Creative Writing & Content Generation

When generating creative content, it's important to specify the **tone, style, and intended audience** to ensure the AI aligns with your expectations.

Example:
✅ *"Write a short, humorous story about a cat who becomes the mayor of a small town."*
(Goal: Creative storytelling with a specific theme.)

✅ *"Generate a professional LinkedIn post announcing our company's expansion into Europe."*
(Goal: Business-related content with a professional tone.)

If you need AI to **mimic a certain tone**, adding descriptions like "humorous," "inspirational," or "formal" helps refine the result.

e) Code Generation & Debugging

For technical use cases like coding, a well-structured prompt ensures Copilot generates **functional and relevant** code.

Example:
✅ *"Write a Python function that calculates the factorial of a number using recursion."*
(Goal: Code snippet for a specific programming function.)

☑ *"Optimize this SQL query for faster performance: [insert query here]."* (Goal: Code improvement.)

By **clearly defining the coding task**, users can get **useful, executable code** rather than vague or incomplete snippets.

3. Avoiding Ambiguity & Improving Clarity

One of the biggest challenges in AI prompting is **ambiguity**—if a prompt is too broad, vague, or lacks necessary details, the AI may struggle to generate an accurate response.

Unclear   **Prompt:**

✖ *"Tell me about marketing."* (Too broad—what aspect of marketing?)

Improved   **Prompt:**

☑ *"Explain the differences between digital marketing and traditional marketing with examples."* (Clear scope and comparison.)

By specifying **which aspect** of a topic to focus on, you avoid **generic or irrelevant** responses.

4. Refining & Iterating for Better Results

Even with a well-structured prompt, the first response might not always be perfect. It's important to **iterate** and **refine** your prompts based on the output you receive.

Example   **of**   **Iteration:**

1. **First prompt:** *"Explain cybersecurity."* (Too broad—response might be too general.)
2. **Refined prompt:** *"Summarize the top five cybersecurity threats businesses face today."* (More focused.)
3. **Further refined prompt:** *"Summarize the top five cybersecurity threats businesses face today and suggest prevention strategies."* (Now includes solutions.)

This iterative process ensures you **narrow down** the AI's focus to generate the most relevant and valuable response.

Conclusion

Understanding the goal of your prompt is **essential for getting high-quality responses** from AI tools like Microsoft Copilot. Whether you need factual information, summaries, structured instructions, creative content, or coding assistance, defining the **purpose, scope, tone, and format** of your prompt significantly improves the accuracy and usefulness of the output. By following best practices and refining prompts iteratively, users can **unlock the full potential of AI-assisted productivity** and obtain responses that align with their needs.

Aligning Prompts with Specific Tasks and Giving Examples

Microsoft Copilot is a powerful AI assistant that can perform a wide range of tasks, but the **quality of its responses** depends heavily on how well the prompt is aligned with the specific task at hand. A well-crafted prompt guides the AI to produce accurate, relevant, and useful responses tailored to the user's needs. Different tasks—whether they involve writing, summarization, coding, or analysis—require different prompt structures. By **understanding how to align prompts with specific tasks**, users can maximize efficiency and obtain the best possible results.

1. Aligning Prompts for Content Creation

When using Copilot for writing tasks—such as drafting emails, blog posts, reports, or marketing content—it's important to specify the **tone, style, format, and target audience**.

Example 1: Writing a Business Email

✅ *"Write a professional email to a client, thanking them for their recent purchase and offering a 10% discount on their next order."* (Goal: Formal and persuasive customer engagement.)

✅ *"Compose a friendly and engaging email inviting employees to the annual company retreat, including details about the venue and activities."* (Goal: Internal company communication with a warm tone.)

If the prompt lacks clarity—such as *"Write an email for a discount."*—the AI may generate a generic or off-topic response. By specifying **context, purpose, and tone**, the output becomes **precise and effective**.

Example 2: Generating a Blog Post

☑ *"Write a 500-word blog post on the benefits of remote work, using a professional but conversational   tone."*
(Goal: Informative content tailored to remote workers and businesses.)

☑ *"Create a fun and engaging social media post about why coffee is essential for productivity,   using   humor."*
(Goal: Engaging social media content with a specific theme.)

Specifying **word count, tone, and intended platform** helps tailor the response to **the right audience and format**.

2. Aligning Prompts for Summarization and Research

When asking Copilot to summarize information, the key is to **define the scope and format** of the summary.

Example 1: Summarizing an article

☑ *"Summarize the key points of this article on AI ethics in 3 bullet points."*
(Goal: Concise and structured summary.)

☑ *"Provide a one-paragraph summary of the latest advancements in AI research from 2023."*
(Goal: Condensed, year-specific update.)

If the prompt is vague—such as *"Summarize this."*—the AI may not know whether to create a short or detailed summary. Adding **specific instructions** ensures the summary meets user expectations.

Example 2: Extracting Research Insights

✅ *"List three key findings from recent studies on the impact of social media on mental health."*
(Goal: Factual insights with a research-based approach.)

✅ *"Compare and contrast the effects of aerobic and anaerobic exercise on cardiovascular   health."*
(Goal: Analytical summary with a focus on comparison.)

By including **action words like 'list,' 'compare,' or 'analyze,'** the AI understands how to structure the response.

3. Aligning Prompts for Data Analysis and Reports

For tasks involving data analysis, **clarity in scope, required format, and key focus areas** is essential.

Example 1: Generating Business Reports

✅ *"Create a report summarizing quarterly sales performance, including key metrics and   trends."*
(Goal: A structured financial summary with relevant insights.)

✅ *"Analyze customer feedback from our recent survey and highlight three key areas for   improvement."*
(Goal: Customer insights with actionable takeaways.)

If the request is **too general**, like *"Tell me about sales."*, Copilot might generate **unfocused or incomplete** insights.

Example 2: Data Interpretation

✅ *"Interpret this dataset on e-commerce sales trends and summarize key findings in two   paragraphs."*
(Goal: A written analysis of data insights.)

☑ *"Generate a table comparing website traffic before and after our recent ad campaign."*
(Goal: Structured data comparison in tabular form.)

Being **specific about the output format**—such as tables, bullet points, or paragraphs—helps Copilot generate more **usable** results.

4. Aligning Prompts for Coding and Debugging

For coding tasks, prompts must include **programming languages, specific tasks, and any constraints** to ensure accuracy.

Example 1: Writing Code

☑ *"Write a Python function that calculates the Fibonacci sequence up to n terms."*
(Goal: A functional code snippet with a defined task.)

☑ *"Generate a JavaScript script that dynamically updates the background color of a webpage every 5 seconds."*
(Goal: A specific front-end development task.)

If the prompt is **too vague**, such as *"Write a Python program."*, Copilot may not know **what kind of program** is needed. Including **specific instructions** ensures a useful response.

Example 2: Debugging Code

☑ *"Fix this Python code that is supposed to reverse a string but throws an error: [insert code]."*
(Goal: AI-assisted debugging with clear context.)

☑ *"Optimize this SQL query to improve database performance."*
(Goal: Performance improvement for a specific coding issue.)

By specifying **the exact issue or desired improvement**, Copilot can provide **targeted coding assistance**.

5. Aligning Prompts for Problem-Solving and Decision-Making

AI can assist in decision-making by generating **pros and cons lists, comparisons, and action plans**.

Example 1: Making Business Decisions

✅ *"List the advantages and disadvantages of outsourcing customer support for a small business."*
(Goal: A structured decision-making guide.)

✅ *"Compare three popular CRM tools and recommend the best one for a startup."*
(Goal: A comparative analysis with a recommendation.)

Adding **words like 'compare,' 'list,' or 'recommend'** ensures the response aligns with **problem-solving needs**.

Example 2: Strategic Planning

✅ *"Develop a three-step plan for launching a new e-commerce website."*
(Goal: A structured action plan.)

✅ *"Suggest five cost-effective marketing strategies for small businesses."*
(Goal: Practical, budget-friendly marketing advice.)

By framing the request as an **actionable task**, Copilot generates **useful, structured** outputs.

Conclusion

Aligning prompts with specific tasks is **key to unlocking the full potential of Microsoft Copilot**. Whether you need **content creation, summaries, coding assistance, data analysis, or strategic advice**, a well-structured prompt ensures **accurate and relevant responses**. The best prompts clearly define the **task, format, and focus area**, avoiding vague or open-ended instructions. By applying these best practices, users can consistently get **high-quality AI-generated responses** tailored to their exact needs.

Step 2: Providing Context and Constraints

Including Background Information to Refine Responses

One of the most effective ways to improve the quality and relevance of AI-generated responses in **Microsoft Copilot** is by providing **background information** within your prompt. AI tools like Copilot generate responses based on the input they receive, meaning the more **context and detail** you provide, the more **accurate and refined** the output will be. Whether you're crafting an email, summarizing an article, or generating code, background details help **reduce ambiguity**, align responses with **specific needs**, and improve overall usefulness.

1. Why Background Information Matters

Without **adequate context**, AI models may generate **generic, vague, or off-topic** responses. Providing background information helps Copilot understand:

- **The specific topic or problem being addressed.**
- **Relevant constraints or conditions.**
- **The intended audience and tone.**
- **Any prior knowledge or assumptions that should be included.**

For example, if you simply ask:
✖ *"Write a product description."*
This prompt is too broad, and Copilot may generate **generic text** that doesn't align with your product's unique selling points.

Instead, adding background details like the product's **name, features, target audience, and tone** refines the response:
☑ *"Write a 150-word product description for a luxury smartwatch with a titanium case, 10-day battery life, and fitness tracking features. Target the description toward professionals and emphasize style and functionality."*

By specifying key details, the AI generates a **more accurate and engaging** product description.

2. Providing Context for Writing and Content Creation

For writing tasks, Copilot benefits greatly from additional background information regarding the **purpose, audience, and required style**.

Example 1: Business Emails

If you need to draft an email, the AI will generate better responses if you provide:

- The recipient's role (e.g., customer, colleague, investor).
- The purpose of the email (e.g., follow-up, introduction, complaint resolution).
- Any key points that must be included.

❌ *"Write a follow-up email."* (Too vague)

✅ *"Write a polite follow-up email to a client who recently inquired about our software. Thank them for their interest, provide pricing details, and invite them to schedule a demo."*

Adding background details ensures the email is **specific, helpful, and effective**.

Example 2: Blog Writing

If you're asking Copilot to write a blog post, provide details such as:

- The main topic and key subtopics.
- The desired tone (formal, conversational, technical, humorous).
- The target audience (business professionals, students, general readers).
- Any key points or references to include.

❌ *"Write a blog about healthy eating."* (Too broad)

✅ *"Write a 700-word blog post about healthy eating habits for busy professionals. Focus on easy meal prep strategies, quick nutritious snacks, and tips for dining out healthily. Use a friendly and motivating tone."*

By including **audience, focus areas, and tone**, Copilot produces a **well-structured and relevant** blog post.

3. Improving AI Responses for Summarization Tasks

When asking Copilot to summarize content, it's crucial to specify:

- The type of content (e.g., article, book, report, meeting notes).
- The desired length of the summary.
- Any specific details that should be emphasized.

✗ *"Summarize this article."* (Lacks clarity)

✓ *"Summarize this 10-page research article on climate change in 200 words. Focus on the key findings and policy recommendations."*

Adding these details ensures Copilot generates a **focused and concise** summary.

4. Refining Responses in Coding and Technical Tasks

When requesting **coding help** from Copilot, background information is crucial for accuracy. If a prompt lacks **specific details** about the programming language, framework, or expected behavior, the response may not be useful.

Example 1: Writing Code

✗ *"Write a login function."* (Lacks details)

✓ *"Write a Python function for a user login system that checks credentials against a database, returns a JWT token upon success, and limits failed attempts to three."*

By specifying **language, functionality, and security requirements**, Copilot can generate **practical and relevant** code.

Example 2: Debugging Code

If you need help debugging, include:

- The full code snippet.
- The specific error message.
- Expected vs. actual behavior.

❌ *"Fix this Python error."* (Too vague)
✅ *"I'm getting a 'TypeError' when trying to concatenate a string and integer in this Python function. How can I fix it?"*

Providing **specific details about the issue** helps Copilot generate **targeted debugging suggestions**.

5. Enhancing Decision-Making and Analysis Requests

When using Copilot for **decision-making support**, giving background information helps ensure insightful responses.

Example 1: Choosing a Business Strategy

❌ *"What's the best marketing strategy?"* (Too general)
✅ *"Our company is a new online bookstore targeting young adults. What are three effective digital marketing strategies to increase brand awareness and sales?"*

By specifying **industry, target audience, and goals**, Copilot tailors its advice to the business's needs.

Example 2: Product Comparisons

If you're asking Copilot to compare products, provide relevant details like:

- The specific products or brands.
- Key features or factors to compare.
- The intended use case.

❌ *"Compare CRM software."* (Too broad)
✅ *"Compare HubSpot, Salesforce, and Zoho CRM based on pricing, features, and ease of use for a small business."*

This refinement ensures the response is **useful and targeted**.

6. Avoiding Generic or Misleading Responses

Without proper context, Copilot may generate responses that are **too broad, incorrect, or misaligned** with your intent.

Example: Requesting a Definition

✗   *"What   is   cloud   computing?"*   (Generic   response)
☑ *"Explain cloud computing to a non-technical audience using simple examples."* (Refined for clarity and relevance.)

Adding **the target audience or desired level of detail** ensures a **better response**.

Conclusion

Providing **background information** in your prompts is **essential** for refining AI-generated responses. Whether you're requesting **content creation, summaries, coding help, decision-making support, or analysis**, the more **specific context** you provide, the better the AI can align its response to your needs. Instead of using vague prompts, adding details about **purpose, audience, format, constraints, and key points** helps **eliminate ambiguity** and results in **highly accurate and useful outputs**. By mastering the art of **context-rich prompting**, users can unlock **the full potential of Microsoft Copilot** and significantly improve their AI-assisted productivity.

Using Constraints such as Word Limits, Styles, or Formats

When working with AI tools like **Microsoft Copilot**, utilizing constraints such as **word limits**, **styles**, and **formats** can significantly enhance the quality and relevance of the AI-generated responses. By introducing specific limitations, users guide the AI to produce outputs that meet their exact needs, whether it's for content creation, data analysis, or technical tasks. Constraints make the interaction more **efficient** and ensure that the AI's output is tailored to fit the required **structure** and **purpose**.

1. The Role of Word Limits in Refined Responses

Setting a **word limit** is one of the simplest and most effective constraints when crafting a prompt. Word limits help ensure that the response remains **concise**, **focused**, and **appropriate for the intended platform**. Whether you need a quick summary or a brief explanation, specifying the desired word count allows Copilot to adhere to a clear structure, avoiding unnecessary elaboration or overly long responses.

Example 1: Writing a Short Summary

❌   *"Summarize   this   article."*
This prompt may lead to an overly lengthy or unfocused response, as the AI doesn't know how brief the summary should be.

✅ *"Summarize this article in 100 words, focusing on the key points and main argument."*
By specifying the word count, you help Copilot generate a **concise** and **focused** summary that sticks to the essential details.

Example 2: Writing a Social Media Post

Social media platforms have **character limits**, making it essential to tailor responses accordingly.

❌   *"Write   a   tweet   about   the   benefits   of   fitness."*
This prompt could generate a response that's too long for Twitter's 280-character limit.

✅ *"Write a tweet about the benefits of fitness in under 280 characters, including a call-to-action."*
By providing a **character limit**, Copilot will generate content that fits the platform's constraints while still conveying the intended message.

In both examples, the **word limit** provides clarity on the **level of detail** the AI should include, ensuring the output is **precise** and **targeted** to the required format.

2. Leveraging Different Styles for Tailored Outputs

Another key constraint is **style**, which refers to the tone, voice, and approach used in a response. The style of the content often depends on the intended audience and the context of the task. Whether the content needs to be **formal**, **casual**, **professional**, or **humorous**, specifying the desired style helps Copilot adjust its output accordingly.

Example 1: Formal vs. Informal Tone

If you need an email for business purposes, the style should be formal, while a blog post or social media update might call for a more conversational approach.

✗   "Write   an   email   to   a   client."
This prompt may result in a generic response that lacks the specific **tone** appropriate for a business setting.

☑ *"Write a formal email to a client, thanking them for their recent purchase and offering   a   10%   discount   on   their   next   order."*
By specifying the **tone** (formal) and **purpose** (thank you and offer), you ensure the email maintains a professional demeanor.

Example 2: Casual Blog Post

If you're writing a blog post for a lifestyle brand, you may want a casual, friendly tone:

✗   "Write   a   blog   post   about   the   importance   of   sleep."
This could result in a neutral, overly academic tone.

☑ *"Write a fun and engaging blog post about the importance of sleep, aimed at young adults,   using   a   conversational   and   light-hearted   tone."*
The inclusion of the **style** (fun, engaging, conversational) guides Copilot to produce content that resonates with the target audience.

By adding **style constraints**, you ensure that the tone of the response aligns with the specific **purpose** and **audience** you are targeting.

3. Formatting Responses to Meet Specific Needs

The **format** of a response often plays a crucial role in how information is consumed and understood. Whether it's a **list**, **table**, **paragraph**, or **bullet points**, providing formatting constraints helps the AI deliver responses that fit the specific **structure** required by the user.

Example 1: Structured Business Report

Business reports, for example, often require a structured approach that includes key sections like an **introduction**, **findings**, and **recommendations**.

❌ *"Write a business report on customer satisfaction."* This prompt is too vague and does not specify the required structure.

✅ *"Write a business report on customer satisfaction, including an introduction, key findings in bullet points, and three actionable recommendations."* By providing **formatting instructions**, such as specifying **sections** and **bullet points**, you ensure that the final response is **clear** and **organized** for professional use.

Example 2: Creating a Comparison Table

When comparing products or services, tables are a great way to organize data.

❌ *"Compare the features of product A, product B, and product C."* This prompt may lead to a general comparison without a clear structure.

✅ *"Compare the features of product A, product B, and product C in a table format, listing price, durability, and warranty."* By specifying the **table format**, the response is more **organized** and visually accessible, allowing for easy comparison of key features.

4. Creating Content for Specific Mediums

Different **mediums** or platforms may require different types of formatting, word limits, and styles. By understanding the constraints of the medium, you can ask Copilot to generate responses that fit the **specific requirements** of that platform.

Example 1: Website Content

For **web content**, the language often needs to be **SEO-friendly** and **concise**, especially for homepage text or product descriptions.

❌ *"Write a product description for a new blender."* This might result in an overly descriptive or lengthy response.

✅ *"Write a concise, SEO-friendly product description for a new blender, focusing on key features like the 10-speed settings, durable stainless steel blades, and ease of cleaning."*
By specifying the **SEO** need and the **focus areas**, the content becomes more **purposeful** and appropriate for an e-commerce setting.

Example 2: Presentation Slides

For a **presentation**, brevity is key, as slides should support spoken points, not replace them.

❌ *"Create slides for a presentation about digital marketing."*
The AI may generate text-heavy slides that are unsuitable for a presentation.

✅ *"Create 5 bullet-point slides for a presentation about digital marketing trends, each with a title and 3-4 concise points."*
By specifying the **slide format**, **bullet points**, and the number of slides, the response becomes more aligned with the presentation's needs.

5. Combining Multiple Constraints for Precision

In some cases, users may need to combine several constraints to achieve the desired output. By combining **word limits**, **styles**, and **formats**, you can create a highly **refined and tailored response**. This multi-layered approach ensures the output not only meets the content requirements but is also structured in a way that makes it easily digestible for the intended audience.

Example: Press Release

A press release requires **formal language**, a **specific structure**, and sometimes a **word limit** to fit within media guidelines.

❌ *"Write a press release about our new product."*
This prompt lacks critical constraints, and the result may not fit professional standards.

✅ *"Write a formal press release about our new product launch, with a headline, 2-3 short paragraphs summarizing the features, and a quote from the CEO. Limit to 300 words."*

By combining **word count**, **tone**, and **format** (headline, quote, paragraphs), Copilot is guided to produce a **professional** and **media-ready** press release.

Conclusion

Using **constraints** like **word limits**, **styles**, and **formats** is an essential strategy to refine AI responses and ensure they meet specific needs. By clearly defining your **expectations**—whether it's keeping content within a set word count, adjusting the tone, or using a particular structure—you help guide the AI to produce **concise**, **engaging**, and **well-organized** outputs. Constraints are not limitations but tools that shape responses to align with your goals, making your interactions with Microsoft Copilot more **efficient** and **effective**.

Examples of Contextualized vs. Non-Contextualized Prompts

When working with AI tools like **Microsoft Copilot**, the distinction between **contextualized** and **non-contextualized** prompts is crucial in shaping the quality and relevance of the response. A **contextualized prompt** provides additional details, background information, and specific requirements, whereas a **non-contextualized prompt** is vague, broad, or lacks critical details. The difference between these two types of prompts can be significant, leading to responses that are either highly relevant and accurate or unnecessarily general and vague. Understanding how to contextualize prompts can help users get better, more tailored outputs for their needs.

1. Non-Contextualized Prompts: General and Broad

A **non-contextualized prompt** is typically one that lacks any kind of **specific information** or **details** about the task at hand. These prompts often lead to broad or generic responses from the AI because the model does not have enough context to understand exactly what the user wants. The results may miss important nuances, be too vague, or not fit the user's intended purpose.

Example 1: Writing an Email

- **Non-Contextualized**   **Prompt:**
  "Write an email to a customer."

This prompt is very vague and does not provide any useful context for the AI to generate a tailored response. The AI has no way of knowing the purpose of the email (e.g., sales inquiry, support request, thank you note), the tone required (formal, friendly, apologetic), or specific details to include (e.g., product information, instructions, offers). As a result, the output may be too generic to effectively communicate the message to the recipient.

Response   **Example:**
"Dear Customer, I hope this email finds you well. Thank you for being a valued customer. If you have any questions, please feel free to ask."
While polite, this email lacks any **specificity** and fails to meet the user's actual needs.

Example 2: Summarizing an article

- **Non-Contextualized**   **Prompt:**
  "Summarize this article."

Without context, the AI does not know the key focus areas, length, or level of detail required for the summary. The user might want a high-level overview, specific sections summarized, or the main findings highlighted. In the absence of this information, the AI may provide a summary that does not prioritize the right points or is too long.

Response   **Example:**
"This article talks about various methods for reducing carbon emissions and discusses the impacts of different strategies. It mentions renewable energy, carbon capture, and public   *policy."*
While the summary covers the general themes, it lacks any depth or focus on the user's desired sections or insights.

2. Contextualized Prompts: Tailored and Focused

A **contextualized prompt** provides enough specific information to guide the AI in crafting a response that meets the user's exact needs. By adding **context**, such as the **purpose**, **audience**, **constraints**, and **desired outcomes**, the user increases the likelihood of receiving an accurate and relevant response. This approach ensures that the AI has a clear understanding of the task and can align its output to suit the user's goals.

Example 1: Writing an Email

- **Contextualized** **Prompt:**
  "Write a formal email to a customer who recently purchased a software product. Thank them for their purchase, provide information on how to access customer support, and offer a 10% discount on their next purchase. Keep the tone polite and professional."

In this case, the user provides clear context: the purpose of the email (thank you for purchase), the desired content (information on customer support and a discount offer), and the tone (polite and professional). This allows the AI to generate a **well-structured** and **targeted response** that meets the user's expectations.

Response **Example:**
"Dear [Customer's Name],
Thank you for your recent purchase of [Product Name]. We hope you're enjoying your new software. Should you need any assistance, our customer support team is available at [Support Contact Information]. As a valued customer, we'd like to offer you a 10% discount on your next purchase. Please feel free to contact us with any further questions.
Best regards,
[Your Company]"

This response is **specific** to the user's request and provides all the necessary details in a **clear and professional manner**.

Example 2: Summarizing an article

- **Contextualized** **Prompt:**
  "Summarize this article in 200 words, focusing on the key findings and implications for climate change policy."

In this case, the user has specified not only the **length** of the summary (200 words) but also the **focus** (key findings and implications for policy). This guidance helps the AI prioritize the most important information and ignore unnecessary details.

Response **Example:**
"The article discusses the impact of rising global temperatures on agricultural productivity, highlighting how crop yields are expected to decrease in certain regions.

It emphasizes the importance of adaptive strategies, such as drought-resistant crops and changes in farming practices, to mitigate the effects of climate change. The author argues that government policies must be enacted to support farmers and encourage sustainable agricultural practices to address the challenges posed by climate change."

The summary is **focused** on the **key findings** and **policy implications**, as requested, and stays within the required word count.

3. The Impact of Contextualized Prompts on AI Performance

Contextualizing prompts not only improves the **accuracy** of the AI's response but also enhances the **efficiency** of the interaction. When users provide context, they are more likely to receive **targeted, actionable, and relevant outputs** that meet their needs. It allows Copilot to avoid **misunderstanding the task** and helps to reduce the need for **further clarification or revision**.

Example 1: Content Creation for a Blog Post

- **Non-Contextualized** **Prompt:**
  "Write a blog post about healthy living."
  Without details about the target audience, the length of the post, or any key points to cover, the AI may create a very general post.

Response **Example:**
"Living a healthy life involves eating well, exercising regularly, and taking care of your mental health. It's important to stay active and eat nutritious foods."

- **Contextualized** **Prompt:**
  "Write a 600-word blog post about healthy living for busy professionals, focusing on quick meal prep ideas, stress management techniques, and efficient exercise routines. Use a friendly, motivating tone."
  By providing **audience** (busy professionals), **focus areas** (meal prep, stress management, exercise), and the **tone** (friendly, motivating), the AI generates a much more **relevant** and **engaging** post that aligns with the user's objectives.

Response **Example:**
"As a busy professional, finding time for a healthy lifestyle can be challenging, but with the right strategies, it's possible to stay fit and energized. One simple way to maintain a healthy diet is by meal prepping on weekends. Pack your meals with lean proteins,

veggies, and whole grains to keep you fueled throughout the week. In addition to diet, managing stress is essential—practice mindfulness techniques, like deep breathing, during your lunch break. And don't forget about exercise! A quick 20-minute workout can boost your mood and energy levels, even if you only have a short window of time."

4. Conclusion: The Power of Contextualization

In summary, the difference between **contextualized** and **non-contextualized prompts** can have a profound impact on the quality and relevance of the AI's responses. **Non-contextualized prompts** are often vague and lack the necessary details for the AI to fully understand the user's needs, leading to generic or unfocused responses. On the other hand, **contextualized prompts** provide the AI with the **specifics**—such as the purpose, audience, constraints, and tone—necessary to generate more accurate, targeted, and actionable outputs. By taking the time to add context to prompts, users can significantly enhance the effectiveness of AI tools like Microsoft Copilot, ensuring they get exactly what they need in the most efficient and relevant manner.

Step 3: Structuring Complex Prompts

Breaking Down Multi-Step Requests

When interacting with AI tools like **Microsoft Copilot**, providing clear and well-structured multi-step requests is essential to ensure that the response is accurate, organized, and meets the user's needs. Multi-step requests, as the name suggests, involve multiple tasks or actions that need to be completed in sequence. These can range from writing, research, or problem-solving tasks that require different phases of execution. Breaking these requests into clear, digestible steps ensures that the AI understands the overall goal while managing individual steps with precision and coherence.

1. The Complexity of Multi-Step Requests

Multi-step requests are inherently more complex than single-step prompts because they require the AI to maintain a **logical flow** of information and actions. If the request is vague or too broad, the AI might struggle to break down the task and address each component adequately. This is particularly true when dealing with **creative tasks** (e.g., writing, content creation) or **analytical tasks** (e.g., data processing, comparisons) that need to be tackled in phases.

In contrast, when multi-step requests are clearly defined and structured, the AI can take a more methodical approach, ensuring that the result aligns with each phase of the task. The goal is to create a roadmap for the AI to follow, reducing the chance of confusion or errors and ensuring a well-rounded, complete output.

2. The Importance of Clarity in Stepwise Instructions

When asking the AI to complete a multi-step task, **clarity** is crucial. It's important to break down each phase of the task into its individual components. If the steps are not sufficiently defined, the AI may produce incomplete, inaccurate, or off-topic responses. Ensuring each step is clear, concise, and provides specific guidance helps the AI understand the relationship between tasks and produce a more coherent output.

Example 1: Writing an article

- **Non-Structured**   **Multi-Step**   **Prompt:**
  "Write an article on climate change, discussing its impact, solutions, and global initiatives."
  While the task seems straightforward, the lack of clarity around the subtopics and structure of the article could confuse the AI. The response may lack focus, or the AI might not effectively separate the individual themes.
- **Structured**   **Multi-Step**   **Prompt:**
  *"Write an article on climate change.
    o Start with an introduction explaining what climate change is.
    o Discuss the major impacts of climate change on the environment.
    o Present solutions for mitigating climate change.
    o End with an overview of global initiatives and their effectiveness."*

This structure clearly breaks down each task, helping the AI address each topic thoroughly before moving on to the next. The result will be an article with distinct sections that cover all requested points systematically.

3. Using Sequential Instructions to Guide the AI

One of the key strategies when issuing a multi-step prompt is to use **sequential instructions**. These are instructions where the AI is guided to perform each task in a set order. Sequential instructions help maintain a **logical flow** and ensure that the AI's output builds on previous steps. The goal is to make sure that each action or step is performed before moving on to the next, allowing the AI to focus on completing one part of the task at a time.

Example 2: Research and Analysis Task

- **Non-Structured   Multi-Step   Prompt:** *"Research the latest trends in digital marketing and write a report on them."* This prompt lacks specificity and might confuse the AI in how to break down the research and report writing process. It doesn't clarify whether the AI should focus on sources, themes, or specific examples.
- **Structured   Multi-Step   Prompt:** *"Research the latest trends in digital marketing.
  - First, search for the top trends in digital marketing for 2025.
  - Then, find reputable sources or studies that discuss these trends in detail.
  - Analyze how these trends are expected to influence businesses.
  - Finally, write a report that includes the trends, their potential impact on businesses, and suggested strategies for companies to adapt."*

In this version, each task is broken down into a logical **sequence**: research, sourcing, analysis, and then writing. By guiding the AI through each stage, the results will be more comprehensive and well-supported by evidence.

4. The Role of Subtasks in Clarifying Multi-Step Requests

Another helpful strategy for breaking down multi-step requests is to use **subtasks**. Subtasks act as smaller, manageable portions of a larger task, helping the AI focus on specific pieces before assembling them into a final output. By breaking complex tasks into **bite-sized pieces**, you reduce the risk of confusion and ensure that the AI can address each subtask independently. This method is especially useful for **problem-solving**, **research**, and **analytical writing**.

Example 3: Business Plan Creation

- **Non-Structured Multi-Step Prompt:** *"Write a business plan for a new online store."* This prompt is too broad, and the AI might struggle to cover all aspects of a business plan (e.g., marketing, finance, operations) in an organized way.
- **Structured Multi-Step Prompt with Subtasks:** *"Write a business plan for a new online store.
  - Write a section describing the business idea, including the target market and product offerings.
  - Create a market analysis section that explains the competitive landscape and potential customer base.
  - Write a marketing strategy section, detailing advertising methods and social media outreach.
  - Create a financial plan, including revenue projections and startup costs.
  - Finally, conclude with a summary of the store's goals and key performance indicators (KPIs)."*

Here, each section of the business plan is broken down into **subtasks**, making it easier for the AI to focus on one component at a time, ensuring a more comprehensive final document.

5. Providing Contextual Support for Each Step

It's important to not only break down tasks but also to offer **context** for each individual step. This helps the AI to understand the scope and depth of each task and ensures it completes the request in line with your expectations. Without the right level of context for each step, the AI may struggle to produce appropriate responses or may produce responses that are irrelevant to the overall request.

Example 4: Design a Marketing Campaign

- **Non-Structured Multi-Step Prompt:** *"Design a marketing campaign for a new fitness product."*

Without further information, the AI might create an incomplete or superficial campaign.

- **Structured Multi-Step Prompt with Contextual Support:** *"Design a marketing campaign for a new fitness product targeting women aged 25-40.
    o Begin with brainstorming campaign slogans that appeal to this demographic.
    o Create a list of digital platforms (social media, blogs, email) where the campaign should be promoted, with reasoning behind each choice.
    o Develop a timeline for the campaign, including key dates for launch and promotional events.
    o Suggest an advertising budget allocation and include justification for spending on each platform."*

By providing **contextual support** for each step—such as the target audience, reasoning behind platform choices, and campaign goals—the AI is better equipped to create a well-rounded, effective marketing campaign.

6. Handling Feedback and Adjusting Steps

In multi-step tasks, it's also important to consider how feedback can be used to adjust or refine the results at each step. Sometimes, users may want to refine certain steps before proceeding to the next. Breaking down the process allows the user to review and provide feedback at each stage, enhancing the overall quality of the output.

Example 5: Report Writing

- **Initial   Prompt:**
  "Write a report on the impact of artificial intelligence in healthcare."
- **Broken   Down   with   Feedback   Opportunity:**
  "1. Research the top applications of artificial intelligence in healthcare.
  2. Provide a summary of the key findings with supporting data and studies.
  3. Draft an introduction with an overview of AI's role in healthcare.
  4. Write a conclusion that offers potential future trends and challenges.
  5. After reviewing, I will provide feedback and ask for any revisions if necessary."

This stepwise approach provides a chance to review each part of the report, offering the ability to fine-tune the content before moving on to the next phase.

Conclusion

Breaking down multi-step requests is an essential skill when working with AI tools like Microsoft Copilot. By dividing a complex task into smaller, more manageable steps, users help the AI maintain focus and consistency throughout the process. Structured prompts with **clear instructions**, **specific sub-tasks**, and **contextual support** ensure that the AI can provide highly relevant, comprehensive, and accurate responses. Whether it's writing, research, or problem-solving, clear and organized multi-step prompts help maximize the efficiency and effectiveness of AI interactions, leading to high-quality outputs tailored to the user's goals.

Using Sequential Prompts for Detailed Outputs

When working with AI systems like **Microsoft Copilot**, one of the most effective ways to ensure detailed, comprehensive outputs is to use **sequential prompts**. Sequential prompts guide the AI through a series of steps, each of which builds on the previous one, allowing for a more detailed and structured response. By breaking down complex tasks into smaller, manageable stages, users can direct the AI to focus on one aspect at a time, ensuring that the final output is thorough, organized, and aligned with their expectations. This approach is particularly beneficial for tasks that require **multi-phase** work, where each stage contributes to the overall result.

1. The Concept of Sequential Prompts

A **sequential prompt** involves a series of prompts that are given in a specific order. Each prompt focuses on a distinct aspect of the task, and the output from one stage informs the next. This method contrasts with a more **general, all-encompassing prompt** that asks the AI to complete the entire task at once, which can often lead to vague or disorganized responses. Sequential prompting breaks the task into steps, with each step receiving focused attention, thereby increasing the likelihood of receiving detailed and accurate outputs.

For example, when writing an article, instead of asking the AI to "write an article about the future of renewable energy," a sequential approach would involve dividing the task into parts, such as:

1. Ask the AI to provide an introduction to renewable energy.
2. Request a discussion of current renewable energy trends.
3. Have the AI examine future possibilities for renewable energy.
4. Finally, ask for a conclusion that ties the findings together.

Each step is distinct, which allows the AI to work through the task in a focused and thorough manner.

2. Why Sequential Prompts Work for Detailed Outputs

Sequential prompts work because they break a **complex task** into smaller, manageable pieces. Each piece is given its own dedicated focus, which ensures the AI can dive deeper into each aspect without becoming overwhelmed or distracted by other components. This method ensures that the AI doesn't overlook key details, providing a more **well-rounded**, **detailed**, and **coherent response**.

For instance, if asked to write a detailed analysis of a **business market**, a general prompt might lead to an output that only touches on high-level insights without diving deeply into specific aspects like **customer segments, competitor analysis, or market trends**. However, by sequentially prompting the AI for each component—one for customer analysis, another for competitor review, and so on—users are more likely to receive a response that covers the **depth** of the topic from all relevant angles.

3. Structured Approach to Complex Tasks

Sequential prompts are particularly useful for tasks that require **structured** and **multi-phase work**, such as:

- **Research-based tasks**: For instance, if a user is asking for an in-depth report, they can sequentially prompt the AI to focus on **research**, **data gathering**, **analysis**, and then **final presentation** of findings. Each phase will be refined and expanded upon before moving on to the next.
- **Creative writing projects**: In the case of a novel, blog post, or any form of long-form writing, sequential prompts guide the AI to write an introduction first, then chapters or sections, and finally, a conclusion. Each part can be reviewed and revised before progressing to the next, ensuring the entire piece is cohesive.

- **Problem-solving tasks**: When tackling complex problems such as **mathematical proofs** or **engineering design**, breaking the task into sequential components allows the AI to focus on each calculation or design element before moving to the next, ensuring accuracy at every stage.

By guiding the AI through the process step-by-step, users maintain control over the flow and content of the output, which is especially important in tasks that require careful thought and organization.

4. Example: Writing a Research Paper Using Sequential Prompts

Let's consider writing a research paper on the **impact of AI on healthcare**. Instead of asking the AI to write the entire paper in one go, sequential prompts allow the user to focus on each section of the paper one at a time. Here's how that could look:

- **Step   1:   Introduction**
  "Provide an introduction to the topic of AI in healthcare. Discuss its potential, recent advancements, and why it is an important subject."
- **Step   2:   Literature   Review**
  "Summarize the key studies on the application of AI in healthcare, focusing on its uses in diagnostics, treatment, and patient care."
- **Step   3:   Impact   Analysis**
  "Analyze how AI is transforming healthcare services, both positively (e.g., improved diagnostics) and negatively (e.g., data privacy concerns)."
- **Step   4:   Future   Prospects**
  "Explore the future of AI in healthcare. What technological advancements are expected in the next decade, and how might they further revolutionize the industry?"
- **Step   5:   Conclusion**
  "Conclude by summarizing the key findings and suggesting directions for future research in the field of AI in healthcare."

This **step-by-step approach** ensures that each section of the paper is developed in detail before moving to the next, which results in a **cohesive, well-researched**, and **comprehensive research paper**.

5. Enhanced Flexibility for Revisions

One of the main advantages of using sequential prompts is the **flexibility** it provides in managing revisions. Since the work is being completed in stages, users can review each section or step of the task before proceeding to the next one. If adjustments are needed, users can simply revise the completed steps and ask the AI to refine the output based on that feedback. This level of flexibility ensures that users can maintain control over the quality and accuracy of the work, making it easier to implement changes and refine the final output.

For instance, if the AI generates a **market analysis** that is too general, the user can prompt it to revisit specific areas of the analysis—such as customer demographics or competitor behavior—before continuing with the next phase of the project. This minimizes the risk of **disjointed outputs** and ensures that each section is tailored to the user's specific requirements.

6. Examples of Sequential Prompts in Action

Example 1: Product Description Creation

If a business needs detailed **product descriptions** for an e-commerce website, a series of sequential prompts can break down the task:

1. *"Provide a brief overview of the product's features and benefits."*
2. *"Describe the materials used to make the product, highlighting any unique or high-quality aspects."*
3. *"Outline the product's target audience and ideal use cases."*
4. *"Suggest potential ways customers can personalize or adapt the product to suit their needs."*
5. *"Write a conclusion that encourages potential customers to purchase the product."*

By breaking the task into these distinct phases, each part of the product description is addressed with sufficient detail, ensuring that the final output is both informative and persuasive.

Example 2: Developing a Marketing Strategy

A sequential approach to creating a **marketing strategy** can also be extremely effective:

1. *"Research the target market, including demographics, behaviors, and key trends."*
2. *"Create a list of marketing channels (e.g., social media, paid ads, influencer partnerships) that are most effective for this market."*
3. *"Develop a content plan, including themes, topics, and types of content to be produced."*
4. *"Estimate the budget allocation for each marketing channel and explain why this allocation is appropriate."*
5. *"Create a timeline for the execution of the marketing campaign, including key milestones and launch dates."*

By tackling each element of the marketing strategy individually, users can ensure that every aspect is developed thoughtfully and in line with their overall objectives.

7. Conclusion: The Power of Sequential Prompts

Using **sequential prompts** is an incredibly powerful technique for eliciting **detailed**, **organized**, and **high-quality outputs** from AI tools. By breaking down complex tasks into manageable steps, users ensure that each aspect of the work is given proper attention, leading to a comprehensive and accurate final result. This approach is particularly useful for tasks that require **multiple phases**, such as **writing projects**, **research assignments**, **analytical tasks**, or **problem-solving exercises**. With sequential prompts, users maintain full control over the flow of the work and can adjust each phase before progressing to the next, ultimately resulting in an output that is **tailored**, **cohesive**, and well-researched.

Leveraging Bullet Points, Numbered Lists, and Keyword Emphasis

When crafting prompts for AI systems like **Microsoft Copilot**, one of the most effective techniques for ensuring clarity and focus is leveraging **bullet points**, **numbered lists**, and **keyword emphasis**. These formatting strategies serve not only to break down complex information into digestible chunks but also guide the AI in structuring its responses in a way that is easily accessible, organized, and aligned with user expectations. Whether you're seeking detailed instructions, a step-by-step analysis, or a list of key takeaways, these tools can help you get the best output from your AI interactions.

1. The Power of Bullet Points

Bullet points are a simple yet powerful way to convey key pieces of information quickly and concisely. They are ideal for presenting lists, outlining main ideas, or highlighting important concepts without overwhelming the reader with long paragraphs. For AI systems, bullet points provide a clear and structured framework to generate responses that focus on individual elements, making it easier to extract specific details or insights from complex prompts.

Bullet points are particularly useful when requesting **summaries** or **high-level overviews**, as they allow the AI to break down large topics into digestible chunks. For example, if you were asking Copilot to provide a summary of a book, you could structure the prompt as follows:

*"Summarize the key themes of the book *1984* by George Orwell using bullet points:

- Discuss the concept of totalitarianism and surveillance.
- Explain the role of language manipulation through Newspeak.
- Outline the impact of individual freedom and conformity."*

This structured format helps the AI target the most important aspects of the book while avoiding irrelevant or excessive detail. Bullet points prompt the AI to focus on the essential elements, leading to concise, effective responses.

2. Numbered Lists for Step-by-Step Guidance

Numbered lists are incredibly useful when the task requires a specific order of operations, or when the user needs to outline steps in a process. These lists provide structure and sequence, making them ideal for **procedural tasks, how-to guides**, and **step-by-step instructions**. Numbered lists ensure the AI focuses on each individual task in order, creating a clear roadmap for delivering an organized and detailed response.

For example, if you're asking the AI to generate a detailed plan for starting a new business, a numbered list can break down the process into manageable steps:

*"Create a step-by-step guide for starting an online business:

1. Conduct market research to identify your target audience and competition.
2. Develop a business plan, outlining your goals, products, and revenue model.
3. Register your business and obtain necessary licenses.

4. Create a website and set up an online store.
5. Develop a marketing strategy to attract customers.
6. Set up financial tracking and ensure accounting practices are in place."*

The numbered structure keeps each phase of the task distinct and clear, ensuring that the AI addresses each step comprehensively. The use of numbers guides the AI to avoid skipping any critical component of the process.

3. Keyword Emphasis for Clarity and Focus

Keyword emphasis plays an important role in highlighting the core elements of a request. By emphasizing key terms or concepts within your prompt, you signal to the AI which aspects of the task are the most important. This can help the AI focus on specific details or themes, ensuring that the response aligns with the user's primary objective.

Keyword emphasis can be achieved in several ways:

- **Bold** or **italicize** keywords to give them visual prominence.
- Use **capital letters** for key terms that you want to highlight.
- Reiterate key concepts by including them multiple times in the prompt.

For example, if you want to generate content around **sustainability** in business, emphasizing this concept in your prompt helps the AI focus on your main topic. Here's how you might structure the prompt:

*"Write an article on how **sustainability** is shaping the future of business:

- What are the key **sustainability practices** businesses are adopting?
- Discuss the role of **sustainability** in supply chain management.
- How does **sustainability** impact long-term profitability and brand reputation?"*

In this example, **sustainability** is emphasized in each question, making it clear that the entire response should revolve around this core theme.

4. Combining Bullet Points, Numbered Lists, and Keyword Emphasis

For even more effective prompting, combining bullet points, numbered lists, and keyword emphasis can create a **highly structured**, **easy-to-follow** prompt that guides the AI through complex tasks with clarity. This method allows users to provide both detailed context and clear directions, enhancing the AI's ability to generate responses that meet specific needs.

Let's say you're asking the AI to create a **content strategy** for a website. By using a combination of these techniques, you can structure your request like this:

*"Create a detailed content strategy for a website focused on **travel and adventure**:

1. **Identify** the target audience and their interests (e.g., solo travelers, eco-tourism).
2. Develop a content calendar with topics and publishing dates.
3. **Keyword research**: Focus on high-volume keywords like **adventure travel**, **solo travel tips**, and **sustainable tourism**.
4. Create 3 sample blog post titles that focus on **adventure travel**.
5. Outline an SEO strategy for each blog post, including the use of **meta descriptions** and **internal linking**."

Here, the combination of **numbered steps** and **keyword emphasis** ensures that the AI focuses on each distinct task in the right order while honing in on important concepts like **target audience** and **keyword research**. This helps the AI provide more detailed and useful outputs.

5. Using Lists to Enhance Readability and Accessibility

Both bullet points and numbered lists enhance the **readability** of a prompt. In complex or long prompts, it's easy for the AI (and the user) to lose focus. Lists, whether they're bullet points or numbered, visually break the information into smaller sections that can be processed more easily.

This is especially important in tasks that require **comprehensive answers** or **elaborate explanations**. For example, when asking for a **product review** or **research analysis**, a structured list can help ensure the AI covers all relevant points, making the response clearer and more structured.

For example, asking the AI to generate a **comparison** of two smartphones might look like this:

*"Compare the features of the **iPhone 16** and **Samsung Galaxy S25**:

- Design and display quality
- Camera specifications and performance
- Battery life and charging capabilities
- Operating system and software features
- Pricing and value for money"*

This breakdown allows the AI to easily address each comparison point in turn, making it easy for the user to review and understand the final output.

6. Using Lists for Scalability and Flexibility

Lists also offer **scalability** when the complexity of a task increases. If a task requires more information than initially expected, it's easy to add extra points or steps to the list, adjusting the prompt accordingly without overwhelming the AI with too much unstructured information at once.

For instance, if you need more in-depth detail about a certain topic (say, **marketing trends** in 2025), you could start with a basic list and then expand it:

*"Outline the **top marketing trends in 2025**:

1. AI-driven marketing tools
2. Interactive and immersive content (AR/VR)
3. Sustainability-focused branding
4. Increased personalization and data-driven strategies"*

If you need further elaboration on one of the points, you can simply adjust the prompt to add more detail:

*"Expand on the point about **AI-driven marketing tools**, focusing on their impact on customer personalization and automation."*

By adjusting a list and expanding on individual points, you maintain clarity and keep the request organized, allowing for more flexible and targeted results.

7. Conclusion: Maximizing Efficiency and Clarity

Leveraging **bullet points**, **numbered lists**, and **keyword emphasis** is a proven strategy for improving the **clarity**, **focus**, and **effectiveness** of prompts when using AI tools like **Microsoft Copilot**. These techniques allow users to clearly define their needs, organize tasks logically, and highlight important elements, ensuring that the AI can produce the most relevant, accurate, and detailed responses. Whether breaking down complex projects into smaller, more manageable steps, or emphasizing key concepts to guide the AI, these strategies improve both the **efficiency** and **precision** of AI-generated outputs. By adopting these methods, users can unlock the full potential of AI in delivering high-quality content that is both structured and comprehensive.

Step 4: Refining and Iterating Prompts

Analyzing Initial Responses for Improvement

When working with AI tools like **Microsoft Copilot**, one of the most important practices for ensuring high-quality results is to analyze the **initial responses** and refine them based on feedback. The first response the AI provides may not always fully meet your expectations in terms of detail, tone, or accuracy. This is where the iterative process of analyzing and improving the AI's output becomes essential. By understanding how to effectively assess the initial response, users can guide the AI toward more relevant, comprehensive, and accurate results.

1. Why Analyzing Initial Responses Is Crucial

The initial response from an AI is often a starting point—an attempt to address the prompt based on its internal model and algorithms. However, **AI models** are designed to generate broad responses that are generalized, and they might not always capture the nuances, specifics, or depth that a user requires. Analyzing the **first draft** allows the user to pinpoint areas where the AI's output is either too vague, too detailed, or off-track entirely. This step is crucial because it sets the stage for **refinement** and **optimization**, ensuring that the AI's responses evolve over time to match your expectations.

For example, if you ask the AI to generate a **summary** of a lengthy research paper, the first draft may capture the general idea but lack critical details or specific findings. By evaluating this response, you can decide what areas need additional focus or clarity, prompting the AI to expand on certain points or refine others.

2. Key Aspects to Focus on When Analyzing Responses

To effectively assess the AI's initial response, it's important to focus on several key aspects. These aspects help identify specific areas of improvement and provide clarity on how to guide the AI for better outputs.

- **Relevance**: Does the response align with the prompt's primary goals? For instance, if you're asking for a **marketing strategy**, is the response focused on actionable strategies, or does it drift into unrelated aspects of the business?
- **Completeness**: Has the AI covered all the necessary points? This includes ensuring that no critical components are missing. For example, in a research paper summary, are all the major findings discussed, or did the AI overlook some key concepts?
- **Accuracy**: Are the facts, data, or concepts presented correctly? If the AI provides incorrect or outdated information, this will need to be corrected. You can ask for **specific clarifications** or **fact-checking** based on the initial output.
- **Tone and Style**: Does the tone of the response match the expected style? For instance, if you're requesting a **formal report**, but the AI generates a conversational tone, this would require adjustments. Similarly, if you're seeking a **creative** response, but the AI is too rigid, prompting it for a more informal style could improve the outcome.
- **Clarity**: Is the response well-structured and easy to follow? Responses may sometimes be **overly complicated** or lack structure, which can reduce their overall effectiveness. By evaluating how clearly the AI presents its ideas, you can ask it to break down its points into smaller, more digestible sections.

3. Common Issues with Initial AI Responses

Even though AI tools like Copilot have become quite advanced, their first responses often contain a few common issues. Being able to identify and address these issues is an essential part of the **refinement process**. Here are some typical challenges:

- **Vagueness or Overgeneralization**: One of the most common issues is that AI responses can be too broad or superficial. For example, if asked about a complex topic like **climate change solutions**, the AI might provide a list of general strategies (e.g., renewable energy, conservation) without diving deeply into how these strategies can be implemented or their specific impacts.
- **Lack of Depth**: Sometimes the AI may provide an adequate **overview**, but fail to go into enough detail on critical points. In such cases, the initial response might seem like a **starting point** but lacks the comprehensive analysis you need. For instance, in a **business plan**, it might highlight the importance of **market research**, but fail to provide actionable steps for conducting the research.
- **Inconsistent Focus**: At times, the AI may wander off-topic or include irrelevant details that aren't aligned with the user's primary request. This can happen if the prompt was too broad or unclear. Analyzing the response helps clarify whether the AI's focus aligns with the desired outcome.
- **Inaccurate Information**: AI is trained on vast amounts of data, but it's still prone to errors, especially if the data it pulls from is outdated or incorrect. For example, if you're asking about the latest trends in **artificial intelligence**, the AI might provide outdated information, necessitating a more accurate and updated response.
- **Tone Mismatch**: Sometimes, the AI's tone doesn't align with the type of output you were expecting. For instance, a request for a **professional email** might result in a casual or overly informal response, requiring a revision to adopt a more **formal, business-like tone**.

4. How to Refine the AI's Response

Once you've identified areas for improvement, you can take several steps to **refine the response**. The process of fine-tuning and making adjustments allows the AI to better meet your needs.

- **Provide Specific Feedback**: The more specific you are when prompting the AI, the better the results will be. Instead of simply asking for a more detailed answer, you can guide the AI with specific instructions, such as, "Can you expand on the section about customer segmentation?" or "Can you include more examples in the conclusion?"
- **Request Additional Details**: If you feel the AI has skipped over an important detail, ask for more information in that area. For instance, if the AI has provided a

high-level overview of a **financial plan**, you might ask, "Can you provide a breakdown of the financial projections for the next three years?"

- **Refocus the AI's Attention**: If the response lacks focus or goes off-track, refocusing the AI by reminding it of key details can help it stay on task. For example, if the AI starts discussing unrelated topics, you might say, "Please focus only on the product launch aspects of the marketing strategy" or "I need more details about the customer experience, not just the technological aspects."

- **Clarify and Simplify**: If the response is **overly complex** or difficult to follow, you can ask the AI to break down its ideas into smaller sections or use simpler language. For instance, if the explanation of a technical process is confusing, a follow-up prompt like "Can you simplify that in layman's terms?" can help.

- **Revise the Tone**: If the tone doesn't align with what you're looking for, you can prompt the AI to adjust it accordingly. Whether it's asking for a more formal tone or a more creative, informal approach, specifying the **tone** helps guide the response. For instance, "Can you make the tone more formal?" or "Please use a more casual, conversational tone."

5. Iterating with Follow-Up Prompts

The process of refining AI responses is often **iterative**, meaning it might take multiple prompts to fine-tune the output to your satisfaction. After providing feedback and receiving a revised response, it's important to **reassess** the new output and determine if it aligns more closely with your expectations. This iterative process ensures that the final output is polished and tailored to your specific needs.

For example, if the AI's first response to a **marketing campaign proposal** isn't detailed enough, you can follow up with requests like:

- "Can you expand more on the digital marketing strategy?"
- "Can you provide a breakdown of the budget allocation for each channel?"
- "Can you include examples of successful campaigns in a similar industry?"

Each follow-up prompt adds layers of depth to the response, refining it until you achieve the desired outcome. This process allows you to transform a **generic response** into a **highly customized**, detailed output.

6. Balancing Precision with Flexibility

While analyzing and improving initial AI responses, it's important to strike a balance between precision and **creative flexibility**. In some cases, overly restrictive requests for precision might limit the AI's ability to generate creative or insightful solutions. On the other hand, being too vague can lead to incomplete or overly general responses.

It's crucial to assess the AI's initial output and determine whether the problem lies in the **precision of the information** or the **overall approach**. For example, if you're asking the AI for an **innovative business idea** but it provides a typical, well-known suggestion, you might need to adjust the prompt to ask for **more originality** or **out-of-the-box ideas**.

7. Conclusion: The Importance of Iteration and Feedback

In conclusion, analyzing initial responses from AI systems is a vital step in the **refinement** process. By assessing the relevance, completeness, accuracy, tone, and clarity of the AI's first draft, users can provide specific, actionable feedback to improve the quality of the output. This iterative process ensures that the AI's responses evolve over time, becoming more tailored, detailed, and aligned with the user's objectives. By actively refining and guiding the AI through multiple prompts, users can harness its full potential and generate highly relevant and customized content.

Adjusting Wording, Specificity, and Scope

When working with AI tools like **Microsoft Copilot**, **GitHub Copilot**, or other similar models, one of the most powerful methods for refining the results is adjusting the **wording**, **specificity**, and **scope** of your prompts. These three factors play a crucial role in shaping the responses you get, allowing you to get more precise, relevant, and actionable output. Adjusting each of these elements can ensure that the AI's responses align better with your needs, whether you're looking for a brief summary, a detailed analysis, or creative input.

1. The Role of Wording in AI Responses

Wording plays a fundamental role in how an AI interprets a prompt. The way you phrase a question or request significantly affects how the model understands and processes the information. Small changes in language can completely alter the direction of the output.

For example, if you ask an AI, "What are some ideas for marketing?" the response could be broad and unspecific, as the term "ideas" is open-ended. However, if you ask, "What are some innovative digital marketing strategies for small businesses?" the model will have a much clearer direction and focus, potentially narrowing the ideas down to specific tools, strategies, or platforms that cater to small businesses.

In general, precise wording minimizes ambiguity, allowing the AI to understand exactly what you're asking. The clearer the language, the better the response. For instance, instead of asking, "Tell me about the benefits of exercise," you could ask, "List three scientifically-backed benefits of regular cardiovascular exercise for heart health." This more specific wording encourages the AI to focus on measurable, evidence-based answers, making the response more actionable.

2. Specificity: Focusing on the Details

Specificity is an essential element in guiding the AI to provide relevant and actionable responses. The more specific your prompt, the more likely the AI will produce responses that meet your expectations. This is particularly important when you need **detailed, nuanced**, or **targeted information**.

For example, if you're requesting advice on **productivity strategies**, a vague prompt like "Give me tips on being productive" may result in a generic list that doesn't fit your context. In contrast, asking "What are some productivity strategies specifically for remote teams using Slack and Zoom?" immediately narrows the scope to strategies that integrate these tools, leading to a much more tailored response.

Similarly, specificity is critical when asking for help with **technical tasks**. If you're asking for help with **coding** and simply request, "Can you help me with my code?" the AI may give generic tips. On the other hand, if you specify, "Can you debug the Python code for data processing where I'm encountering a ValueError?" the AI will know exactly where to focus its efforts, providing more targeted and relevant suggestions.

Moreover, being specific about what you're **not** asking for can also help the AI filter out irrelevant responses. If you're asking for feedback on a **marketing proposal**, you could say, "Give feedback on the digital channels used in this marketing proposal, excluding social media strategies," which guides the AI to focus only on what you need.

3. Adjusting Scope: Narrowing or Expanding Requests

Scope refers to the breadth of the topic or task you're asking the AI to address. Adjusting the scope of your prompt helps you control the level of detail and the overall **breadth** of the AI's response.

A **narrow scope** can be beneficial when you're looking for deep insights into a specific topic. For example, if you need an **analysis of recent trends in AI**, you could adjust the scope to focus on a particular aspect: "What are the recent advancements in AI related to natural language processing in 2024?" This adjustment narrows the AI's focus to a single aspect of AI, ensuring the response is more detailed and current.

On the other hand, a **broader scope** may be useful when you're looking for a general overview or need to explore multiple areas within a topic. If you're asking for information about **artificial intelligence**, a broad prompt like, "Give me an overview of AI technologies," will likely lead to a more general response that covers the various subfields like machine learning, computer vision, robotics, and natural language processing.

Adjusting scope also helps when you're dealing with large or complex tasks. If you're asking for a **business plan** and want to focus on just the marketing aspect, narrowing the scope could look like this: "Provide a marketing strategy for a new online apparel business, excluding finance and operations sections." This ensures the AI generates a focused output that meets your needs, without veering into other aspects that are outside of your request.

4. The Balance Between Specificity and Scope

In practice, **specificity** and **scope** often need to be balanced for the best results. Too much specificity can lead to overly narrow responses that miss the bigger picture, while too broad a scope can result in responses that are vague and lack depth.

For example, imagine you are asking for advice on **business growth strategies**. If your prompt is "Provide strategies for business growth," it's too broad, and the AI might offer generic strategies like **cost-cutting** or **new product offerings**. However, asking, "Provide a business growth strategy for an online retail business in the fashion industry focusing on customer retention," narrows the scope and adds specificity to the request, but might exclude other important factors like market expansion or product diversification.

On the other hand, a prompt like, "What are the customer retention strategies for e-commerce businesses?" is specific enough to get targeted responses while still allowing for a range of tactics, such as loyalty programs, email marketing, or user experience enhancements. By balancing specificity with scope, you give the AI enough direction to stay focused but leave room for creative and detailed responses.

5. Practical Examples of Adjusting Wording, Specificity, and Scope

Let's walk through a few practical examples to demonstrate how adjusting wording, specificity, and scope can impact the AI's response.

- **Example 1: Wording Adjustment**
    - Broad prompt: "Tell me about sustainability."
    - Adjusted prompt: "Provide an overview of sustainable business practices that companies can adopt to reduce their environmental footprint."

In this example, changing the wording from a vague question to one that specifies **business practices** makes the AI more likely to focus on relevant strategies and initiatives related to sustainability.

- **Example 2: Specificity Adjustment**
    - General request: "What are some digital marketing trends?"
    - Adjusted request: "What are the top digital marketing trends for B2B businesses in the tech industry in 2025?"

Here, adjusting the **specificity** by mentioning **B2B** and **tech industry** narrows the scope, ensuring that the AI's response is more relevant to a particular business context.

- **Example 3: Scope Adjustment**
    - Broad prompt: "Give me advice on improving my website."
    - Adjusted prompt: "Provide advice on improving my website's user interface to enhance the user experience."

By narrowing the scope from **general advice** to **user interface** specifically, the AI is more likely to focus on design, layout, and usability improvements rather than more general website enhancements like SEO or content strategy.

- **Example 4: Combining Specificity and Scope**
  - General prompt: "Explain how AI is used in healthcare."
  - Adjusted prompt: "Explain how AI is used to diagnose diseases using medical imaging technologies like MRI and CT scans."

In this case, both **specificity** (AI use in diagnostics) and **scope** (medical imaging technologies) have been adjusted to create a prompt that leads to a more focused and actionable response.

6. The Benefits of Adjusting Wording, Specificity, and Scope

By adjusting the wording, specificity, and scope of your prompts, you can achieve multiple benefits:

- **Precision and Relevance**: More specific prompts help the AI focus on the most relevant areas, ensuring that the output is aligned with your needs.
- **Clarity**: Clear wording reduces ambiguity, preventing the AI from misinterpreting your request or providing a generic response.
- **Depth**: Adjusting specificity allows you to dive deeper into particular aspects of a topic, rather than getting a superficial, broad response.
- **Efficiency**: A well-adjusted prompt will generate a more accurate and targeted response on the first try, saving time and reducing the need for revisions.

7. Conclusion: Refining Your Prompts for Optimal AI Output

In summary, adjusting the **wording**, **specificity**, and **scope** of your prompts is essential for optimizing the AI's response to meet your needs. By carefully considering how you phrase your requests, how much detail you include, and how broad or narrow the subject matter should be, you ensure that the AI produces **relevant**, **detailed**, and **accurate** outputs. This iterative approach to prompt design helps you harness the full potential of AI tools, turning them into powerful resources that can support a wide range of tasks, from generating content to solving complex problems.

Using Feedback Loops to Enhance Results

In the realm of AI-assisted productivity, particularly when using tools like **Microsoft Copilot** or **GitHub Copilot**, **feedback loops** are a fundamental practice for refining and enhancing the output. By continually assessing the AI's initial responses and providing targeted feedback, you can significantly improve the quality, relevance, and accuracy of the results. This process of refining AI-generated outputs through feedback is essential in transforming initial drafts into highly tailored, actionable, and effective content. Understanding how to create and leverage feedback loops allows users to guide the AI through a continuous improvement cycle, ultimately optimizing its performance over time.

1. What is a Feedback Loop?

A feedback loop refers to the process of **providing feedback** on an initial output and using that feedback to adjust future responses. In the context of AI, this involves providing the AI with input on how it performed in the previous step, whether it's a matter of accuracy, tone, style, specificity, or depth. Based on this feedback, the AI adjusts its next response to better align with the user's expectations and goals.

For example, if you ask the AI for a detailed report on a marketing campaign and the first draft is too high-level, you might respond by saying, "Please include more detailed metrics and case studies in the analysis." The AI then processes this feedback and generates a more comprehensive report in the next iteration. This back-and-forth process of feedback and revision is what constitutes a feedback loop.

2. Importance of Feedback Loops in AI-Driven Workflows

Feedback loops are critical for improving the quality of AI responses over time. Without this iterative process, the AI might continue to produce results that are either too general, inaccurate, or out of alignment with the user's needs. Here are some reasons why feedback loops are so important in AI-driven workflows:

- **Refinement**: The first response from an AI model is rarely perfect. Through feedback, the AI can refine its understanding of what is needed and adjust future responses to be more in line with the user's expectations. Feedback allows the AI to fine-tune its approach and get closer to the desired outcome with each iteration.
- **Adaptability**: AI models like Microsoft Copilot and GitHub Copilot are designed to adapt based on the user's guidance. A well-designed feedback loop helps the AI

model learn what the user needs in specific contexts, making it more flexible and responsive to different tasks.

- **Personalization**: The more feedback you provide, the more the AI can tailor its responses to your **unique preferences**. Over time, this customization leads to better results, as the AI adapts to your specific needs and style.
- **Accuracy and Relevance**: Feedback helps the AI focus on the most important aspects of a task, eliminating irrelevant content and honing in on the areas that matter most. For example, if you ask for information on a highly specialized topic and the AI provides irrelevant data, feedback ensures it focuses more on the core aspects of your request.

3. How Feedback Loops Work in Practice

The process of using feedback loops with AI tools typically follows a **cyclical pattern** that involves a few key steps:

- **Initial Prompt**: You start by giving the AI a specific, well-defined prompt. This is the baseline for the output.
- **First Response**: The AI generates a response based on its understanding of the prompt. This output might be detailed or high-level, depending on how well the prompt was constructed and how the AI interprets it.
- **Analysis**: You assess the first response. Does it meet your expectations? Is it too vague, inaccurate, or off-track? Are there areas where it could be more detailed or better structured?
- **Provide Feedback**: Based on your analysis, you provide the AI with feedback. This can involve asking for more information, adjusting the tone, narrowing the scope, or adding clarity to the initial request. For instance, if the AI's response is too generic, you could prompt, "Can you provide more specifics about X?" or "Expand this section with concrete examples."
- **Refinement**: The AI processes the feedback and generates an updated response. It uses the feedback to improve on the previous draft, making necessary adjustments in terms of content, tone, or structure.
- **Repeat the Cycle**: This process continues until the AI delivers the desired result. The more you iterate and provide feedback, the closer the AI's output will come to meeting your needs.

4. Types of Feedback to Provide

The effectiveness of a feedback loop relies on **specificity and clarity**. Vague or overly general feedback won't provide the AI with clear guidance on what needs to change. Below are different types of feedback that can be used to enhance results:

- **Clarification of Scope**: If the response goes off-topic or doesn't fully address your needs, you can clarify the scope of your request. For example, "Focus more on the **financial** aspects rather than marketing strategies" or "Can you narrow the analysis to only address the latest trends in AI for 2024?"
- **Request for More Detail**: If the initial response is too superficial, you can ask the AI to **expand on specific points**. For example, "Can you provide more examples of the strategies you mentioned?" or "Please elaborate on the potential impact of these trends in the next five years."
- **Tone Adjustment**: Sometimes the tone may not align with the intended output. You can ask for the response to be more formal, casual, or professional based on the context. For example, "Make the tone more formal" or "Adopt a conversational style with a friendly tone."
- **Accuracy and Precision**: If there are factual errors or vague statements, providing feedback like, "The statistics in the second paragraph are outdated. Can you update them with the latest data?" helps the AI focus on delivering more accurate and relevant content.
- **Structure and Format**: Sometimes, the output may lack the necessary structure. You can ask for specific formats or organized sections. For example, "Please list the key points in bullet points" or "Break the content into two sections: introduction and conclusion."

5. Iterating for Better Results

One of the most powerful aspects of feedback loops is the ability to iterate until the output meets your needs perfectly. Through multiple rounds of feedback, the AI is able to fine-tune its responses based on your continuous input.

For example, imagine you're using an AI tool to write a **product description**. The first response might be too generic, so you ask for more details about the features and benefits. After the second attempt, you find that the tone still isn't aligned with your brand's voice, so you adjust the feedback again. Over several rounds, the AI's output improves, becoming increasingly closer to the desired product description.

The iterative nature of feedback loops helps ensure that each output is more refined than the last, resulting in highly customized and accurate content. This allows users to unlock the full potential of AI, enhancing its value over time.

6. Benefits of Using Feedback Loops for AI Optimization

Using feedback loops to enhance AI responses provides several clear benefits, especially in professional or business contexts where **accuracy**, **relevance**, and **personalization** are key.

- **Continuous Improvement**: The iterative process allows the AI to improve its performance over time. Each round of feedback serves to **teach** the AI about your preferences, leading to better-tailored responses in future iterations.
- **Customization**: By providing specific feedback about tone, style, detail, and focus, you ensure that the AI adapts its responses to your unique requirements. This **personalized approach** can significantly improve productivity, saving time on revisions and improving the output quality from the start.
- **Consistency**: Feedback loops help maintain **consistency** in AI outputs, ensuring that responses align with your desired standards across multiple tasks. Whether it's in **marketing content**, **technical writing**, or **creative projects**, iterative refinement ensures that the AI continuously delivers high-quality, consistent results.
- **Efficiency**: The feedback loop process ultimately saves time. While the initial responses may need adjustments, the refinement cycle accelerates after each iteration. You avoid having to start from scratch and can fine-tune existing responses more efficiently.

7. Conclusion: Mastering the Art of Feedback Loops

In conclusion, using **feedback loops** is an essential practice for refining and improving the output of AI models like **Microsoft Copilot** and **GitHub Copilot**. By analyzing the first response, providing targeted feedback, and iterating over multiple cycles, users can enhance the quality of AI responses, making them more accurate, relevant, and customized to specific needs. The ability to guide AI through this **continuous improvement process** not only helps in achieving the desired outcome but also empowers users to unlock the full potential of AI tools. As AI continues to evolve, leveraging feedback loops will remain one of the most effective strategies for maximizing productivity and creativity.

Step 5: Leveraging Copilot for Specific Use Cases

For Coding: Writing Effective Prompts for GitHub Copilot

GitHub Copilot is a powerful tool designed to assist developers by suggesting code snippets, completing functions, and even generating entire blocks of code based on natural language prompts. However, to unlock its full potential, it's important to craft **effective prompts**. How you ask GitHub Copilot to generate code can significantly impact the quality, accuracy, and usefulness of its suggestions. This section explores the key principles for writing effective prompts when using GitHub Copilot, allowing developers to improve productivity and get more precise and relevant results.

1. Understanding GitHub Copilot's Capabilities

GitHub Copilot is built on **OpenAI's Codex** model, which can understand natural language and generate code in response to requests. It supports a wide range of programming languages, frameworks, and libraries. However, the model isn't perfect—it responds best when it receives clear, detailed, and contextual prompts. A vague or ambiguous request may result in less useful or even incorrect code. As such, understanding Copilot's capabilities and limitations is crucial to writing effective prompts.

GitHub Copilot is especially adept at:

- **Auto-completing code**: It can predict the next line of code based on the context provided.
- **Function generation**: You can describe a function in natural language, and Copilot will attempt to write the corresponding code.
- **Refactoring and debugging**: By providing specific requests, such as "Refactor this code to make it more efficient," Copilot can suggest optimizations or identify potential errors.

To get the best results, it is essential to provide clear instructions, relevant context, and specific requests that guide the AI toward a suitable solution.

2. Writing Clear and Specific Prompts

When using GitHub Copilot, the more **specific** and **clear** your prompts, the more likely you are to get accurate code suggestions. If you want Copilot to write a function, you need to outline what the function should do, what parameters it should take, and what the expected output is. Vague instructions like "write a function" are unlikely to yield satisfactory results.

Example of a vague prompt:

- "Write a function that does something with numbers."

This request lacks essential information and context, making it challenging for Copilot to generate useful code. A more detailed prompt, on the other hand, gives Copilot clear instructions to follow.

Example of a more effective prompt:

- "Write a Python function that takes a list of integers and returns the sum of all the even numbers in the list."

Here, the prompt is clear, specific, and describes exactly what the function should do. Copilot will have a much higher chance of generating an accurate function that meets the user's requirements.

3. Providing Context for Complex Problems

GitHub Copilot's responses improve when it is given relevant **context** about the code it is generating. This is especially true for **larger projects** or more **complex functions**. When asking Copilot to generate code for specific tasks, such as integrating with an API, working with a database, or building a machine learning model, it's important to include context like the technologies or libraries being used, any relevant dependencies, and the overall goal of the task.

Example without context:

- "Create a function that processes user data."

This is too ambiguous, and without context, GitHub Copilot cannot know which kind of user data is involved, how to process it, or what libraries to use.

Example with context:

- "Create a Python function using Pandas that reads a CSV file of user data and processes the age column by normalizing the values between 0 and 1."

This version of the prompt provides **specific details**: the technology (Python, Pandas), the task (reading a CSV), and what should be done with the data (age column normalization). Copilot can now generate code that is more accurate and suited to the task.

4. Leveraging Comment-Based Prompts

GitHub Copilot is highly responsive to **comments** within your code. Writing comments in natural language can give Copilot a clear idea of what you're trying to achieve, and it will attempt to generate code based on those instructions. This approach is especially useful when working on larger projects or when collaborating with others.

Example of using comments to write prompts:

```python
CopyEdit
# Write a function that takes a string as input and returns the number of vowels in the string.
def                                     count_vowels(input_string):
    pass
```

Here, the comment clearly specifies the function's task. Copilot will attempt to generate a Python function that processes the string and counts the vowels.

Another way to refine Copilot's output is by writing more detailed comments at each step of the code. You can outline what each function should do, and Copilot will attempt to fill in the gaps.

Example:

```python
CopyEdit
# Define a class that represents a Book with attributes: title, author, and pages.
class                                                                        Book:
    pass

# Add a method to the Book class that calculates the reading time based on an average
reading            speed            (pages            per            hour).
```

By providing these prompts within the comments, Copilot understands the context and will generate corresponding code for both the class definition and its method.

5. Asking for Refactoring or Optimizing Code

GitHub Copilot can also help with **refactoring** or **optimizing** existing code. By providing specific prompts about improving the code's efficiency, readability, or structure, you can guide Copilot to suggest changes. This can be particularly useful when dealing with legacy code or when looking to improve the performance of a function.

Example of a prompt asking for refactoring:

- "Refactor this function to make it more efficient by reducing the time complexity."
- "Rewrite this function to improve readability and add comments explaining each step."

Here, Copilot will aim to analyze the existing function and suggest changes that optimize performance or improve readability.

6. Debugging with Copilot

GitHub Copilot can also assist in **debugging** by analyzing the code and suggesting fixes for errors or issues. To get the best debugging suggestions, it's essential to include clear instructions about the error or bug you're encountering.

Example of a vague debugging prompt:

- "Fix the error in this function."

This prompt doesn't give enough detail for Copilot to understand the exact issue. It's more effective to describe the error you're facing.

Example of a more effective debugging prompt:

- "This Python function throws a TypeError when passed a string. Can you fix the error and ensure the function handles different data types?"

The added context about the specific error (TypeError) and the goal of handling different data types helps Copilot generate a more accurate fix for the issue.

7. Combining Multiple Prompts for Complex Tasks

In situations where a task is more **complex** and involves multiple steps or components, you can break down the request into **sequential prompts**. This way, Copilot can generate solutions for each part of the task, and you can combine those solutions later.

Example of a multi-step prompt sequence:

1. **Prompt 1:** "Create a Python function to fetch data from a REST API using the requests library."
2. **Prompt 2:** "After fetching the data, parse the JSON response and return a list of names."
3. **Prompt 3:** "Sort the list of names alphabetically and return the first 10 results."

By breaking down the task into sequential prompts, Copilot can handle each individual aspect, ensuring that the code is generated in manageable chunks, each focusing on a single part of the problem.

8. Testing Copilot's Suggestions

Even when GitHub Copilot generates code that seems correct, it's always important to **test** the generated code to ensure it works as expected. Writing effective prompts also involves **checking the AI's outputs** and using them as a foundation to iterate upon.

Example of a testing prompt:

- "Write a test case using unittest to verify that the count_vowels function correctly counts the vowels in different strings, including edge cases like empty strings or strings without vowels."

Through this approach, GitHub Copilot will generate not just code but a corresponding test case to ensure that the function performs correctly.

9. Improving Code Quality with Style Guidelines

If your project follows specific **coding style guidelines**, you can ask GitHub Copilot to generate code that adheres to those standards. This can include naming conventions, formatting, and code structure.

Example of a style request:

- "Write a Python function that follows PEP 8 guidelines and includes type hinting for all function arguments and return values."

By including a style request in your prompt, Copilot will generate code that is not only functional but also aligns with industry-standard practices.

10. Conclusion: Mastering GitHub Copilot for Coding

Writing effective prompts for GitHub Copilot is about **clarity**, **context**, and **specificity**. The better your prompt, the more relevant and accurate the suggestions Copilot will generate. By including clear details about the task at hand, providing context, and iterating on the feedback from Copilot, you can enhance the AI's responses to meet your coding needs. Whether you're writing new code, refactoring existing functions, debugging errors, or testing new solutions, effective prompting is key to maximizing the power of

GitHub Copilot and improving your coding workflow. By mastering the art of prompt engineering, developers can boost their productivity, streamline their coding tasks, and produce high-quality code more efficiently.

For Business Documents: Crafting Prompts for Emails, Reports, and Presentations

In today's fast-paced business environment, efficiency and clarity are key when it comes to communication. Microsoft Copilot and other AI tools offer tremendous assistance in generating business documents, including emails, reports, and presentations, saving professionals time and ensuring consistent, high-quality outputs. However, the effectiveness of these AI-generated documents relies heavily on how well the user crafts the prompts. In this section, we explore how to write effective prompts for emails, reports, and presentations to maximize productivity and ensure your communication is professional and impactful.

1. Crafting Prompts for Emails

Emails are one of the most common forms of business communication, and crafting effective email prompts for AI tools like Microsoft Copilot can save valuable time while maintaining a high level of professionalism. When creating an email prompt, the more detail you provide, the more relevant and tailored the response will be.

A. *Writing a Professional Email*

A well-written email should convey its message clearly, with a tone that matches the context of the situation. Whether it's a formal business inquiry or a casual follow-up, providing specific information in your prompt helps the AI generate the right response.

Example of a vague prompt:

- "Write an email to a client."

This prompt lacks key details such as the purpose of the email, the relationship with the client, and the desired tone. To improve it, add relevant context:

Example of an effective prompt:

- "Write a formal email to a client apologizing for a delayed delivery. Include an explanation of the issue, a new expected delivery date, and an assurance of improved service moving forward."

Here, the AI will generate an email that covers all necessary components: an apology, an explanation, a new timeline, and an action to restore customer confidence.

B. Following Up on an Email

Another common email task is following up on previous correspondence. Whether you're reminding someone about a deadline or checking in on the progress of a request, your prompt should specify the action you expect.

Example of a vague prompt:

- "Write a follow-up email."

This prompt does not clarify the purpose or the recipient's role in the context of the follow-up. Here's a more effective prompt:

Example of an effective prompt:

- "Write a polite follow-up email to a colleague reminding them about the upcoming meeting on Friday and asking if they need any materials for the presentation."

The more information you provide about the context and the goal of the email, the more useful the AI's response will be.

2. Crafting Prompts for Reports

Business reports are essential for conveying information clearly and concisely. Whether you're writing a status update, a quarterly review, or an analysis of a particular project, writing effective prompts for reports ensures that the content generated is on target and useful.

A. Writing a Status Report

A status report provides an overview of the progress of a project or task. It typically includes sections such as progress, challenges, and next steps. To craft an effective prompt, be specific about the report's sections and the type of information you need.

Example of a vague prompt:

- "Write a status report on the marketing campaign."

While this might be a good starting point, it's too general. You need to provide specific parameters to get a more targeted output.

Example of an effective prompt:

- "Write a status report on the marketing campaign, including the current progress of social media ads, any challenges faced, results from the first month, and the next steps for the upcoming quarter."

This prompt ensures the AI covers important components, such as progress, challenges, results, and next steps, and provides a clear framework for the report.

B. Writing an Annual Business Report

For larger and more comprehensive reports, like annual business reviews or performance reports, your prompt should specify the key areas of the report, such as financials, performance, and strategic goals.

Example of a vague prompt:

- "Write an annual report for the company."

This is too broad, and AI might generate an output that lacks important information or specific sections. To improve this prompt, provide the AI with more structure.

Example of an effective prompt:

- "Write an annual report for the company. Include the financial summary, key performance indicators (KPIs), major achievements, challenges faced, and strategic goals for the next fiscal year."

This clear structure allows the AI to understand the important aspects of the report and deliver a more focused and comprehensive result.

3. Crafting Prompts for Presentations

Creating business presentations is another area where Microsoft Copilot and similar AI tools can save time and ensure your messaging is clear and effective. Whether you're presenting to senior leadership, stakeholders, or potential clients, the quality of the presentation is crucial.

A. Writing a Presentation Outline

For a presentation, AI can assist in generating outlines, suggesting bullet points, and providing content for each slide. When crafting a prompt, it's important to be clear about the structure and purpose of the presentation.

Example of a vague prompt:

- "Create a presentation on company performance."

While this prompt asks for a presentation on an important topic, it's too open-ended. The AI needs more specifics to provide useful content.

Example of an effective prompt:

- "Create a presentation outline on company performance for the last fiscal year. Include sections for financial results, growth strategies, key achievements, and future plans for the next quarter."

This prompt provides clear sections that allow the AI to generate a cohesive outline with the appropriate content for each slide.

B. Writing Slide Content

Once you have the outline, the next step is to generate content for each slide. Be specific about the message you want to convey in each section, as well as the style or tone you'd like.

Example of a vague prompt:

- "Write content for the financial results slide."

This lacks context, making it difficult for the AI to generate targeted content. A more specific request would lead to better results.

Example of an effective prompt:

- "Write content for the financial results slide, summarizing total revenue for the year, a comparison with the previous year, and the main drivers behind the growth or decline."

By specifying the content and providing relevant details, the AI can generate clear, accurate, and tailored content for each slide.

C. Tailoring the Tone for Different Audiences

Another important consideration when writing prompts for presentations is ensuring the tone is appropriate for the audience. Whether you are addressing a group of executives or a team of employees, the tone and language used in the presentation should match the setting. Be sure to include this information when crafting your prompts.

Example of a vague prompt:

- "Create a presentation on market trends."

This does not specify the audience, so the AI may generate a tone that is either too technical or too simplistic.

Example of an effective prompt:

- "Create a presentation on market trends for a board meeting. The tone should be formal and professional, with a focus on data and high-level insights."

Including details about the audience and tone allows the AI to better align the content with the expectations of your audience.

4. Reviewing and Refining Generated Content

After receiving the AI-generated draft for emails, reports, or presentations, it's crucial to review and refine the output. While AI can provide a solid foundation, human input is still necessary to ensure that the document reflects the company's unique voice, adheres to internal standards, and is free of errors.

- **For emails**, ensure that the tone is consistent with your brand and that all necessary details (such as dates or contact information) are included.

- **For reports**, check the accuracy of the data presented and ensure that the structure aligns with your company's reporting standards.
- **For presentations**, make sure the slide content flows logically and that the visuals (graphs, charts, etc.) align with the text.

By reviewing and refining the AI-generated content, you can ensure the final product is polished and ready for professional use.

5. Conclusion: Mastering Prompts for Business Documents

In summary, crafting effective prompts for AI tools like **Microsoft Copilot** to generate business documents is an essential skill for professionals. Whether writing emails, reports, or presentations, the key to getting useful results lies in being specific, providing context, and tailoring your requests to the task at hand. Clear prompts help the AI produce accurate, relevant, and high-quality content that meets your business needs, saves time, and improves productivity. With practice, you can become adept at using AI to assist with your business communication, making your workflow more efficient and ensuring your documents are consistently professional.

For Content Creation: Generating Blogs, Marketing Copy, and Creative Writing

In the ever-evolving world of content creation, the demand for fresh, engaging, and high-quality materials is constant. Content creators—whether they are bloggers, marketers, or creative writers—often face challenges when it comes to producing ideas, maintaining consistency, and overcoming writer's block. However, the advent of AI tools, such as **Microsoft Copilot** and other AI-driven platforms, has revolutionized the content creation process by providing invaluable assistance. These tools can help generate blogs, marketing copy, and creative writing with remarkable speed and creativity. To fully harness their potential, it's important to craft clear and effective prompts that guide the AI in producing content that aligns with your goals.

1. Generating Blog Posts with AI

Writing blog posts can be a time-consuming process, requiring both creativity and research. With AI, the task can be made more efficient. AI can assist in generating blog ideas, drafting sections, or even writing full-length articles, all while maintaining relevance and engaging tone. However, the key to obtaining the best results lies in crafting specific prompts that outline your blog's purpose, target audience, and key message.

A. Choosing a Topic and Structure

When generating a blog post, providing clear guidelines about the **topic**, **tone**, and **structure** of the article is essential. A vague prompt such as "Write a blog about technology" could lead to an overly broad or generic piece, but a well-structured prompt will ensure that the content is tailored to your audience and goals.

Example of a vague prompt:

- "Write a blog about technology."

While the topic is clear, it lacks focus and direction. The AI needs more context about what aspect of technology you're interested in, who the target audience is, and the purpose of the blog.

Example of an effective prompt:

- "Write a blog post for a tech-savvy audience about the impact of AI on job automation in 2025. The tone should be informative, with examples from current industries like manufacturing and customer service."

This prompt gives the AI clear direction: the topic, audience, tone, and scope. The AI can now generate an article that directly addresses the concerns of a specific audience, with clear examples and up-to-date information.

B. Generating Sectional Content

Sometimes, content creators need help generating specific sections of a blog post, such as an introduction, conclusion, or subheading content. These pieces of the blog often require attention to detail and a creative touch, which AI tools can assist with.

Example of a vague prompt:

- "Write an introduction to a blog post on digital marketing."

This request is too broad to produce a focused and meaningful introduction. It's more effective to include details about the angle, the problem being addressed, or the target audience.

Example of an effective prompt:

- "Write an engaging introduction for a blog post aimed at small business owners who are just starting with digital marketing. Mention the importance of having an online presence and how it can lead to growth."

By specifying who the audience is, what problem they are trying to solve, and what the introduction should convey, the AI can generate more specific, tailored content that aligns with your goals.

2. Crafting Marketing Copy with AI

Marketing copy is essential for any business, from product descriptions to email newsletters and ad copy. The success of a marketing campaign often depends on how well the copy resonates with the audience and drives them to take action. AI-powered tools can be an incredible asset in generating persuasive, compelling marketing copy—if the prompts are designed well.

A. Writing Product Descriptions

Product descriptions must highlight the features and benefits of the item while appealing to the target audience's emotions or solving a problem. Crafting an effective prompt for product descriptions requires a good understanding of the product and the buyer's persona.

Example of a vague prompt:

- "Write a product description for a blender."

This is too general. To produce more engaging and targeted content, the AI needs more specific details about the blender, its target audience, and the benefits it offers.

Example of an effective prompt:

- "Write a persuasive product description for a high-performance blender designed for health-conscious individuals. Highlight its powerful motor, versatility for smoothies, soups, and nut butters, and its easy-to-clean design."

This prompt includes details about the target audience, product features, and the key benefits that will appeal to potential buyers, making the resulting copy more targeted and persuasive.

B. Writing Ad Copy

Writing concise, compelling ad copy is an essential skill for any marketer. The goal is to grab the audience's attention quickly and encourage them to act. AI can assist by generating ad copy for various platforms (such as Google Ads or Facebook) based on your objectives.

Example of a vague prompt:

- "Write an ad copy for a fitness app."

This is too general. To get more tailored results, provide specifics about the app's features, benefits, and the desired action.

Example of an effective prompt:

- "Write an ad copy for a fitness app targeting busy professionals. Highlight its customizable workout plans, ability to track progress, and short, 20-minute workouts that can be done at home. Include a call-to-action to download the app today."

By specifying the audience, key features, and a clear call to action, the AI is able to generate an ad that will appeal to the right demographic and increase the likelihood of engagement.

3. Generating Creative Writing with AI

Creative writing, such as short stories, poems, and other forms of imaginative content, can also benefit from AI assistance. While AI can't replace the unique voice of a human writer, it can help with idea generation, character development, plot twists, and even sentence structures. Writing effective prompts for creative content requires more flexibility but still benefits from clear guidelines about tone, style, and plot.

A. *Writing a Short Story*

When generating a short story, the AI can help create compelling narratives, but you need to provide some structure to guide it. You may want to specify the genre, main characters, setting, and theme, or let the AI take the lead with a more open-ended prompt.

Example of a vague prompt:

- "Write a short story."

This prompt is too broad and does not specify the genre, characters, or the kind of story the creator is aiming for.

Example of an effective prompt:

- "Write a short story in the mystery genre. Set it in a small coastal town where a detective must solve the case of a missing person. Include a plot twist in the end, revealing a hidden connection between the detective and the suspect."

With this prompt, the AI understands the genre, setting, tone, and even the desired plot twist, leading to a more compelling narrative.

B. *Writing Poetry*

Poetry can be more abstract, but AI tools can still help by offering ideas, starting points, and even full poems. The key to generating good poetry with AI is providing clear constraints—such as the theme, style, and structure you want the poem to follow.

Example of a vague prompt:

- "Write a poem."

This lacks direction and could result in a disjointed or uninteresting piece. It's better to provide some focus, such as the type of poem and the emotion you want to convey.

Example of an effective prompt:

- "Write a haiku about the changing seasons, focusing on the beauty of autumn and the arrival of winter. Use sensory language to describe the cool breeze and falling leaves."

This prompt specifies the type of poem, its theme, and the mood it should evoke, leading to a more focused and meaningful result.

C. Developing Characters or Plot Ideas

For writers who are developing characters or working on a plot, AI can help generate ideas that kickstart the creative process. By giving the AI a clear prompt about the character's backstory, motivations, and challenges, you can get helpful suggestions for character development.

Example of a vague prompt:

- "Write a character description."

This doesn't give much information about what the character is meant to represent or how they fit into the overall story.

Example of an effective prompt:

- "Write a character description for a 40-year-old detective who recently lost their spouse and is dealing with guilt while solving a new case. They are determined, methodical, but emotionally distant."

This prompt provides clear context about the character's age, role, emotional state, and motivations, which will help the AI generate a more detailed and well-rounded character.

4. Refining and Editing Generated Content

Even though AI tools can help with initial content creation, refining and editing the output is an essential part of the process. After the AI generates a draft, it's important to:

- **Review for clarity and coherence**: Ensure that the ideas flow logically and that there are no ambiguities in the content.
- **Ensure accuracy and fact-checking**: AI-generated content might include errors or outdated information. Always verify facts, particularly when writing reports, marketing materials, or blog posts.

- **Polish the tone and style**: Depending on your target audience, you may need to adjust the tone or writing style to fit the context better.

5. Conclusion: Empowering Content Creation with AI

In conclusion, AI tools like **Microsoft Copilot** offer an invaluable resource for content creators, whether you're working on blogs, marketing copy, or creative writing. Crafting effective prompts is key to maximizing the AI's potential to generate content that aligns with your needs. By providing clear, detailed instructions, content creators can leverage AI to boost their productivity, overcome writer's block, and produce high-quality content more efficiently. Whether you're drafting a blog post, crafting marketing materials, or developing creative works, AI tools can be a valuable assistant in your content creation journey.

V. Common Pitfalls and How to Avoid Them

Overly Vague or Ambiguous Prompts: The Challenges They Present in AI-Assisted Content Creation

In the world of AI-assisted content creation, the effectiveness of the generated output heavily depends on the clarity and specificity of the prompts provided. A prompt serves as the foundation of the interaction between the user and the AI. When prompts are overly vague or ambiguous, the AI often struggles to provide a useful, targeted, or high-quality response. Instead, it may produce generic, off-target, or irrelevant results, leading to frustration for users who expect tailored content. Understanding the risks associated with vague or ambiguous prompts is crucial for anyone looking to get the best results from AI-driven platforms like **Microsoft Copilot** and similar tools.

1. The Nature of Vague or Ambiguous Prompts

A vague prompt is one that lacks specificity or clarity, offering minimal guidance to the AI about the context, desired tone, or output structure. On the other hand, an ambiguous prompt is one where multiple interpretation are possible, which can lead to the AI choosing the wrong path. These types of prompts do not provide enough direction for the AI to produce the most relevant or effective response.

For instance, consider the following example:

Vague Prompt Example:

- "Write something about customer service."

This prompt is extremely broad. It does not specify what aspect of customer service the user is interested in—whether it's customer service best practices, the importance of customer service, or a specific issue related to customer service in a particular industry. As a result, the AI may produce a generic, unfocused response that may not meet the user's needs.

Similarly, an ambiguous prompt such as:

Ambiguous Prompt Example:

- "Write a report on employee performance."

This could be interpreted in several ways. Is the user asking for a report on how well employees are performing overall? Or is the focus on the performance of a specific team or department? Are specific metrics or KPIs needed? Without clarifying these details, the AI might generate a report that misses the key points the user is looking for or even generate an output irrelevant to the task.

2. The Risk of Low-Quality Outputs

When prompts are vague or ambiguous, the AI often falls back on generalized knowledge and lacks the nuanced understanding required to produce high-quality, focused content. For example, in the case of vague prompts for blog writing, the AI might provide basic or boilerplate content that doesn't stand out or resonate with the target audience. The response might lack depth or be too generic, and as a result, the content fails to meet the specific needs of the user.

Consider a scenario where a marketer asks for:

Vague Prompt Example:

- "Write a blog about digital marketing."

This is a very broad prompt, and the AI could generate a general piece that touches on various aspects of digital marketing—SEO, social media, email marketing, etc. However, it might not address the specific audience or solve a particular pain point that the marketer has in mind. The lack of context or focus means that the AI might not dive deep into relevant trends, data, or advice that could help the blog stand out in the crowded digital marketing space.

For businesses, this can result in missed opportunities. Content that doesn't cater to the specific target audience or lacks depth in its analysis won't drive engagement, reduce bounce rates, or convert visitors into customers.

3. The Problem of Ambiguous Language and Multiple Interpretations

An ambiguous prompt can lead to unintended results because the AI has to choose between several possible interpretations. Without clear direction, the AI may not focus on the most relevant or useful interpretation for the user's needs. This creates inefficiencies and may necessitate multiple iterations of the same task.

Ambiguous Prompt Example:

- "Write an email about a new product."

This prompt leaves too much open for interpretation. For example, what new product is the user referring to? Is the email meant for customers, potential investors, or internal employees? Should the tone be formal or casual? What key selling points should be highlighted? The AI might generate a generic product announcement email that doesn't align with the specific objectives or tone that the user intends.

When a prompt is ambiguous, it can result in content that lacks focus, making it more difficult for the user to adjust or refine the result afterward. For marketers, this could mean wasting time revising the generated copy to better fit the target audience and brand voice, which leads to inefficiency in the content creation process.

4. Missed Opportunities for Customization and Personalization

One of the key advantages of using AI in content creation is its ability to tailor content to specific needs, styles, and goals. However, vague and ambiguous prompts undermine this capability. The more precise the input, the more personalized and customized the output will be. When users fail to include enough details in their prompts, the AI cannot apply the necessary filters or parameters that would help refine the content to better suit the user's needs.

For example, a prompt such as:

Vague Prompt Example:

- "Write a marketing email."

is not likely to include personalized touches such as addressing the recipient by name, tailoring the message to a specific product or service, or aligning the tone with the company's branding guidelines. If the user had instead provided a more specific prompt:

Effective Prompt Example:

- "Write a personalized marketing email for a subscription-based meal delivery service targeting busy professionals. Highlight the convenience, affordability, and health benefits of the service, and include a call to action for a 10% discount for first-time customers."

This allows the AI to focus on what matters most for the specific audience and product, ensuring the message resonates with potential customers. When prompts are overly vague, the AI can't tap into these crucial details, which could lead to missed engagement opportunities.

5. Inefficiency and Time Wasting

Vague or ambiguous prompts often result in inefficiency. The AI may generate multiple responses that require additional refinement or clarification, which can lead to wasted time. Instead of receiving a polished, targeted result right away, the user may find themselves in a back-and-forth loop, providing feedback to correct the AI's responses. This undermines the purpose of using AI to streamline workflows, particularly for time-sensitive projects.

For instance, a marketer asking:

Vague Prompt Example:

- "Create social media posts."

This could lead to AI generating posts for various platforms (Facebook, Instagram, Twitter, etc.), each with different tone and formats. Some posts may be too formal, while others might miss the key brand message. The user would then have to refine each one manually, effectively turning a quick task into a multi-step process.

An improved prompt would help narrow the AI's focus, allowing for faster and more targeted results:

Effective Prompt Example:

- "Create a series of three Instagram posts for a fashion brand. Focus on promoting a new spring collection. The tone should be casual and aspirational, highlighting the use of eco-friendly materials."

This reduces the need for revisions, leading to a more efficient and effective process.

6. How to Avoid Overly Vague or Ambiguous Prompts

To avoid the pitfalls of vague or ambiguous prompts, there are several strategies you can implement:

- **Be Specific**: Always include key details such as the desired outcome, the audience, the tone, and any necessary constraints. The more context you provide, the better the AI can align its response with your goals.
- **Clarify the Objective**: Clearly state what you want to achieve with the output. Whether it's to inform, persuade, or entertain, this will guide the AI in adopting the appropriate tone and focus.
- **Break Down Complex Requests**: If you have a multifaceted request, break it into smaller parts. For example, rather than asking for a full report in a single prompt, request an outline first and then move on to individual sections.
- **Ask for Examples**: If the AI is unsure of the format or style you're looking for, you can request examples of previous work or content as part of the prompt.

By providing clear, detailed, and structured prompts, you ensure that the AI produces high-quality, relevant content that requires minimal revision. This maximizes both efficiency and output quality, allowing you to focus on the creative or strategic aspects of your work.

7. Conclusion: The Impact of Clear Prompts on AI Effectiveness

In conclusion, overly vague or ambiguous prompts can significantly hinder the effectiveness of AI-driven content generation. These types of prompts lead to suboptimal results, inefficiency, and missed opportunities. By being specific, clear, and detailed in your prompts, you unlock the full potential of AI, enabling it to produce tailored, focused content that meets your needs. When users take the time to craft precise and well-structured prompts, they ensure a smoother interaction with AI tools and achieve better, more effective outputs in a shorter amount of time.

Providing Conflicting Instructions: How It Affects AI Responses and How to Avoid It

When using AI-powered tools like **Microsoft Copilot**, the quality of the responses heavily depends on the clarity and consistency of the prompts provided. One of the most common issues that lead to poor or confusing outputs is the inclusion of **conflicting instructions** within a single prompt. Conflicting instructions force the AI to make assumptions about which directive to prioritize, often leading to unpredictable, inaccurate, or unusable results. Understanding how conflicting prompts affect AI responses—and learning how to avoid them—can significantly improve the efficiency and effectiveness of AI-generated content.

1. What Are Conflicting Instructions?

Conflicting instructions occur when a prompt includes two or more directives that contradict each other. This forces the AI to either ignore one of the instructions, attempt to merge them in an incoherent way, or generate a response that does not fully satisfy any of the given conditions.

For example, consider the following prompt:

Example of Conflicting Instructions:

- *"Write a one-paragraph summary of our new product launch but make it at least 500 words long."*

This request is logically impossible—the AI cannot create a one-paragraph summary while simultaneously meeting a 500-word requirement. In this case, the AI will either:

1. Choose one instruction and ignore the other (e.g., generating a 500-word response but not in a single paragraph).
2. Attempt a compromise (e.g., generating an overly long paragraph that is difficult to read).
3. Provide a response that seeks clarification rather than fulfilling the task.

Such conflicting prompts lead to confusion and inefficiencies, requiring multiple revisions and refinements before a useful response is obtained.

2. How Conflicting Instructions Affect AI Output

When an AI encounters conflicting instructions, it must determine how to prioritize them. However, AI does not have human-like reasoning capabilities to ask clarifying questions or infer the user's true intent in a complex way. Instead, it follows a probability-based approach, often leading to one of the following issues:

a) Partial Compliance with Instructions

The AI may follow one part of the prompt while disregarding another. For example:

Conflicting Prompt:

- *"Write a formal business email with a friendly and casual tone."*

Here, "formal" and "casual" are contradictory tones. The AI might:

- Prioritize formality and deliver a structured but impersonal email.
- Favor a casual tone, making the email too informal for a business setting.
- Produce a confused hybrid that doesn't fully satisfy either requirement.

b) Overly Generic or Neutral Responses

When the AI detects contradiction, it might avoid making a strong decision, resulting in a watered-down or neutral response. Instead of choosing between opposing instructions, it may generate vague content that doesn't fully align with any one directive.

For example:

Conflicting Prompt:

- *"Create a humorous press release about a serious security update."*

Since humor and security are at odds in tone, the AI might default to a neutral, uninspired press release that lacks both humor and seriousness, failing to meet the user's intent.

c) Unusable or Nonsensical Output

In cases where the AI cannot determine a logical way to reconcile conflicting instructions, it may produce an output that appears disjointed, contradictory, or outright incorrect.

For example:

Conflicting Prompt:

- *"Generate a step-by-step tutorial in a single sentence."*

Since tutorials typically require multiple steps and explanations, while a single sentence is too short to convey detailed information, the AI may produce an unreadable run-on sentence or a list of steps that does not fit within one sentence.

3. Examples of Common Conflicting Instructions and Their Pitfalls

Below are some common examples of conflicting instructions, along with the problems they introduce:

Conflicting Prompt
"Write an informal and highly techni guide on data encryption."
"Summarize this article in two senten but ensure it's highly detailed."
"Write a persuasive email, but do not tak strong stance."
"Create a long, in-depth blog post with 200-word limit."

These contradictions force the AI to make choices that may not align with the user's actual intent.

4. How to Avoid Conflicting Instructions in AI Prompts

To get the best results from AI tools like **Microsoft Copilot**, it's important to craft **clear, consistent, and logical prompts**. Here are some strategies to avoid conflicting instructions:

a) Define Your Primary Objective Clearly

Before writing a prompt, identify the most important goal of your request. If multiple objectives exist, consider whether they logically align. For example, if you need both brevity and detail, a better prompt might clarify the balance:

✓ Good Prompt:

- *"Summarize this article in two sentences while highlighting the main argument and key takeaway."*

Instead of asking for an impossible combination (detailed yet short), this clarifies that the summary should focus on essential points.

b) Separate Multiple Requests Instead of Combining Them

If you need content that meets conflicting requirements, break it into multiple prompts or steps.

✕ Conflicting Prompt:

- *"Write a concise yet detailed summary of our annual report."*

✓ Improved Approach:

1. *"Write a concise summary (under 100 words) of our annual report."*
2. *"Now, expand on the summary to include key financial highlights in detail."*

This approach allows the AI to provide both types of content separately without contradiction.

c) Use Conditional or Prioritization Language

If you have multiple conditions but some are more important than others, explicitly state the priority.

✓ Good Prompt:

- *"Write a blog post on remote work trends. Prioritize a professional tone, but allow slight casual elements to make it engaging."*

This helps the AI understand that professionalism is the primary tone, with some flexibility for casual phrasing.

d) Avoid Contradictory Adjectives

Be mindful of adjectives that oppose each other. Instead of using contradictory descriptors (e.g., "formal yet relaxed"), clarify what you actually need.

✓ Good Prompt:

- *"Write a professional yet approachable business email introducing our new product."*

By using **"approachable"** instead of **"relaxed,"** the instructions are clearer and less contradictory.

5. Conclusion: Ensuring Clarity in AI Prompts

Providing conflicting instructions in AI prompts can lead to inefficient workflows, inaccurate outputs, and wasted time refining responses. AI tools rely on clear and logical directions to generate meaningful content. By carefully crafting prompts with **consistent, structured, and prioritized instructions**, users can maximize the effectiveness of AI-assisted content creation.

When using **Microsoft Copilot** or similar AI tools, always review your prompts to ensure they do not contain contradictions. If necessary, **break down complex requests, prioritize objectives, and use clear phrasing** to guide the AI toward the most relevant and useful responses. By refining how prompts are structured, users can harness the full power of AI for more accurate and efficient results.

Expecting Copilot to Generate Perfect Responses Without Iteration: Why Refinement is Essential

AI-powered tools like **Microsoft Copilot** have revolutionized productivity, assisting users in generating text, code, business documents, and creative content quickly. However, one of the biggest misconceptions about AI assistance is the expectation that **Copilot will generate a perfect response on the first attempt**. While Copilot is highly advanced, it is not infallible—it requires **iteration, refinement, and user feedback** to produce the most accurate and useful results. Understanding the importance of an **iterative approach** helps users maximize Copilot's potential and achieve high-quality outputs.

1. AI is a Tool, not a Mind Reader

One of the most fundamental reasons why expecting perfect responses from Copilot is unrealistic is that AI does not "know" exactly what the user wants **unless it is explicitly stated**. Unlike human assistants, who can infer meaning from past experiences, tone, and context, Copilot relies entirely on the **prompt** it receives at any given moment.

For example, if a user requests:

✖   **Vague**   **Prompt:**
"Write a business report on market trends."

Copilot may generate a general market trends report, but the output might not align with what the user had in mind—perhaps they needed trends for a **specific industry, geographic region, or target audience**. The AI isn't at fault here; it simply did not have enough **guidance or constraints** to tailor its response effectively.

✓ **Refined Prompt (After Iteration):** *"Write a 500-word business report on current e-commerce market trends in North America, focusing on mobile shopping behavior and emerging technologies."*

This refined prompt **provides context, scope, and specificity**, significantly improving the quality of the response.

2. AI Responses Are Based on Probability, Not Absolute Truth

Copilot, like other AI models, generates text based on **patterns and probabilities** rather than human reasoning or personal expertise. This means that:

- Some responses may **lack nuance** or **miss critical details**.
- The AI might **default to generic language** if the request is too broad.
- The information generated could **benefit from fact-checking and refinement**.

For example, if a user asks Copilot to:

✗ **Unrealistic Expectation:** *"Write a flawless executive summary of our Q4 earnings report."*

Copilot might provide a well-structured response, but it is unlikely to perfectly match **the exact tone, financial specifics, or insights** the user needs **without review and revision**. A better approach is to treat the AI's output as a **draft or starting point** that requires human oversight and adjustment.

✓ **Best Practice:**

1. **Use Copilot to generate an initial draft.**
2. **Review and refine**—adjust numbers, tone, and industry-specific language.
3. **Iterate based on specific needs** (e.g., shorter summary, more emphasis on a certain aspect).

This approach acknowledges **Copilot's strengths**—speed and structure—while mitigating its limitations by **integrating human judgment and expertise**.

3. The Power of Refinement: Why Iteration is Key

AI-generated responses are rarely **perfect on the first attempt**, but they can **improve significantly with feedback and refinements**. An iterative approach allows users to:

- **Fine-tune content** by adjusting wording, length, and style.
- **Correct inaccuracies** by reviewing and adding human insights.
- **Optimize for clarity and impact** by specifying tone, structure, or audience.

For instance, when generating **marketing copy**, the first AI-generated version might be **too generic** or **lack persuasive elements**. Instead of discarding the output, users can **modify the prompt and regenerate**:

First   Attempt:
"Write   an   ad   for   a   new   fitness   app."
👉 *Result: Generic description about the app's features.*

Refined   Attempt:
"Write a high-energy, persuasive ad for a new fitness app targeting young professionals. Highlight the convenience of short 20-minute workouts, the AI-powered personalized training,   and   the   limited-time   30%   discount   for   new   users."
👉 *Result: More engaging and persuasive copy with clear selling points.*

This iterative process ensures **higher-quality content** by allowing **incremental improvements** instead of relying on Copilot to produce a perfect output immediately.

4. Adjusting Expectations: AI as a Collaborative Partner

Rather than expecting Copilot to **replace human creativity or decision-making**, users should view it as a **collaborative partner** that enhances productivity. Just as a writer edits multiple drafts of an article or a developer refactors code for efficiency, Copilot's outputs **benefit from revision and improvement**.

This collaborative approach applies across various tasks:

- **For Coding:** Developers may need to tweak Copilot's suggestions, optimize efficiency, or fix logical errors.
- **For Business Writing:** Copilot can draft emails, reports, and presentations, but human refinement ensures alignment with company branding.
- **For Content Creation:** AI can generate blog posts, but users must edit for accuracy, flow, and engagement.

By embracing this mindset, users set **realistic expectations** and get **better results** through active engagement rather than passive reliance.

5. Strategies for Effective AI Iteration

To maximize Copilot's effectiveness, follow these best practices:

a) Start with a Clear but Flexible Prompt

- Instead of expecting perfection, **view the first response as a rough draft**.
- Provide **specific details** but remain open to adjusting them based on results.

b) Review and Identify Areas for Improvement

- Check for **clarity, tone, accuracy, and relevance**.
- If the response is too broad or too specific, adjust and refine.

c) Use Follow-Up Prompts to Fine-Tune

- Instead of rewriting from scratch, **ask Copilot to refine**:
  - *"Make this more persuasive."*
  - *"Condense this into three sentences."*
  - *"Adjust this to sound more professional."*

d) Iterate Until You Reach the Best Output

- Think of AI as a process, not a one-time interaction.
- If needed, break complex tasks into **sequential prompts** to get more refined results.

6. Conclusion: AI is Powerful, But Human Oversight is Essential

While **Microsoft Copilot** is a highly capable AI assistant, **expecting perfect responses without iteration is unrealistic**. AI-generated content is only as good as the prompts and **refinement processes** applied to it. By adopting an **iterative approach**, users can transform rough drafts into polished, high-quality outputs that truly meet their needs.

Rather than seeing AI as a **one-and-done solution**, view it as a **collaborative tool**—one that requires **guidance, feedback, and continuous improvements**. By refining prompts, analyzing initial responses, and making targeted adjustments, users can unlock **Copilot's full potential**, making it a valuable partner in productivity and creativity.

VI. Advanced Techniques for Power Users

Using Chain-of-Thought Prompting for Complex Reasoning

AI models like **Microsoft Copilot** can handle a wide range of tasks, from generating simple text responses to tackling complex reasoning problems. However, when dealing with **multi-step logic, detailed analysis, or intricate problem-solving**, a simple prompt is often insufficient. This is where **chain-of-thought (CoT) prompting** becomes a valuable technique. By breaking down complex reasoning tasks into sequential steps, **CoT prompting** allows AI to provide more accurate, structured, and insightful responses.

In this article, we'll explore **what chain-of-thought prompting is, why it's useful, and how to apply it effectively** when using Microsoft Copilot for complex problem-solving.

1. What is Chain-of-Thought Prompting?

Chain-of-thought prompting is a technique in which users guide AI step-by-step through a reasoning process, rather than expecting a complete answer in a single response. Instead of asking for **an immediate solution**, the user **breaks down the request**

into logical steps, encouraging the AI to work through the reasoning in a structured manner.

For example, instead of prompting:

✖   **Basic**   **Prompt:**
"What is the best pricing strategy for a new SaaS product?"

A CoT approach would explicitly guide Copilot through different factors:

✓   **CoT**   **Prompt:**
*"Let's analyze the best pricing strategy for a new SaaS product step by step.

1. Identify the key pricing models for SaaS businesses.
2. Compare their advantages and disadvantages.
3. Consider market trends and competitor pricing.
4. Provide a recommendation based on these factors."*

By instructing Copilot to **reason step by step**, the response is likely to be **more detailed, logical, and accurate**, rather than a vague or overly simplified answer.

2. Why Chain-of-Thought Prompting Improves AI Reasoning

AI models generate responses by predicting likely text sequences based on prior training data. However, **when faced with complex reasoning tasks**, they can sometimes skip crucial steps or oversimplify conclusions. **CoT prompting mitigates these issues** by:

☑ **Encouraging structured thinking** – Forces AI to consider intermediate steps rather   than   jumping   to   conclusions.
☑ **Improving accuracy** – Breaking down reasoning prevents errors caused by missing key   details.
☑ **Enhancing transparency** – Users can follow the AI's logic and adjust prompts if needed.
☑ **Reducing ambiguity** – Instead of an AI-generated guess, CoT provides a thought-out response.

For example, in a **financial decision-making scenario**, asking for a direct answer might result in **generic** or **unsubstantiated** advice. But by **forcing Copilot to work through its reasoning**, the output becomes more reliable.

3. When to Use Chain-of-Thought Prompting

CoT prompting is especially useful for:

a) Mathematical and Logical Problems

When solving a complex equation or making a data-driven decision, breaking down the steps ensures that the AI doesn't make assumptions.

Example:
"Solve for X in the equation: 2X + 5 = 15. Explain each step."

This forces Copilot to show its work rather than skipping to the final answer.

b) Business Strategy & Decision-Making

Analyzing a business case, pricing model, or investment opportunity benefits from CoT prompting because **multiple factors need consideration**.

Example:
"Analyze whether Company X should enter the electric vehicle market. Consider market demand, competitor analysis, supply chain constraints, and profitability."

By listing multiple angles, you **guide** Copilot toward a **thorough** response.

c) Coding & Debugging

When writing or troubleshooting code, Copilot can be more effective if it walks through its approach.

Example:
"Debug this Python script step by step. Identify potential errors and suggest fixes."

This ensures Copilot **explains its logic**, making it easier to validate suggestions.

d) Creative Writing & Content Generation

Even in creative writing, CoT can help generate structured narratives.

Example:
*"Develop a short story outline with these steps:

1. Define the protagonist and setting.
2. Introduce the conflict.
3. Develop the climax.
4. Provide a resolution."*

This **ensures a logical flow** rather than a random or incomplete story.

4. How to Effectively Use Chain-of-Thought Prompting

To apply CoT prompting successfully, follow these **best practices**:

Step 1: Frame the Question Clearly

A vague question leads to a vague answer. Instead, structure your prompt **as a sequence of steps**.

☑ **Good** **Prompt:**
"Analyze the pros and cons of hybrid work environments by considering employee productivity, cost savings, and work-life balance."

This forces Copilot to **think in stages** rather than provide an unstructured answer.

Step 2: Use Numbered or Bullet-Pointed Steps

Breaking down reasoning into **explicit steps** helps Copilot structure its response properly.

☑ **Example** **Prompt:**
*"Evaluate whether social media advertising is effective. Provide your response in these steps:

1. Explain the benefits of social media advertising.
2. Discuss potential drawbacks.
3. Compare it with other digital marketing strategies.
4. Give a final recommendation."*

This structure **ensures completeness and depth** in the AI's answer.

Step 3: Ask for Justification

Encouraging Copilot to **explain its reasoning** improves response quality.

✅ **Example** **Prompt:**
"Compare the effectiveness of email marketing vs. influencer marketing. Explain your reasoning for each, including factors like audience engagement, cost, and ROI."

This avoids **shallow comparisons** and ensures **data-backed insights**.

Step 4: Iterate & Refine

If the initial response lacks detail or skips a step, **follow up with more specific questions** to refine the output.

🔄 **Example** **Follow-Up** **Prompt:**
"Expand on the challenges of influencer marketing, especially regarding trust and long-term brand impact."

This **deepens** the AI's response and ensures a **comprehensive** answer.

5. Conclusion: Unlocking AI's Full Potential with CoT Prompting

Using **chain-of-thought prompting** transforms Microsoft Copilot from a **simple text generator** into a **powerful reasoning assistant**. By breaking down complex problems into **structured steps**, users can guide the AI toward more **accurate, logical, and insightful responses**.

Key **takeaways:**
✓ CoT prompting enhances accuracy by forcing step-by-step reasoning.
✓ It's ideal for complex tasks like business strategy, coding, decision-making, and creative writing.
✓ Well-structured prompts improve AI comprehension and output quality.
✓ Iterating and refining responses ensures depth and completeness.

Rather than expecting AI to **"magically"** produce perfect results in one attempt, leveraging **CoT prompting** makes AI **smarter, more useful, and more aligned with human thinking**. By mastering this technique, users can **harness Copilot's full potential** for tackling complex challenges with confidence. 🚀

Applying Role-Based Prompting: Enhancing AI Responses with Context-Specific Roles

AI models like **Microsoft Copilot** are designed to assist users across various domains, but their responses can vary significantly depending on how they are prompted. One powerful technique to improve the **quality, relevance, and accuracy** of AI-generated content is **role-based prompting**. By assigning the AI a specific role—such as a business consultant, software engineer, historian, or marketing strategist—you can **guide its responses** to better align with your needs.

In this article, we will explore **what role-based prompting is, why it is useful, and how to effectively apply it** when using Copilot for diverse tasks.

1. What is Role-Based Prompting?

Role-based prompting is a technique where the user explicitly instructs the AI to assume a specific identity, profession, or expertise before responding. This approach helps shape the AI's tone, depth of knowledge, and response structure to better suit the given task.

For example, instead of using a **generic prompt** like:

✕   **Basic**   **Prompt:**
"Explain cloud computing."

A **role-based prompt** would provide more clarity and expertise:

✓   **Role-Based**   **Prompt:**
"You are a cloud computing specialist. Explain cloud computing to a group of IT professionals, focusing on scalability, security, and cost-efficiency."

By framing the AI as an **expert** in a specific role, it generates a response **tailored to the audience and context** rather than a generic definition.

2. Why Role-Based Prompting Improves AI Responses

Role-based prompting **significantly enhances AI-generated content** by:

☑ **Increasing specificity** – The AI provides responses that align with professional knowledge and industry best practices.

☑ **Improving tone and style** – A role-based prompt influences whether the response is formal, technical, persuasive, or educational.

☑ **Enhancing depth and detail** – AI models adapt their explanations to fit the assigned expertise level.

☑ **Reducing ambiguity** – The AI understands **who it is speaking as and to whom it is speaking**, leading to more precise responses.

For example, a **finance-related question** can yield very different answers depending on the assigned role:

♦ **As an Economist:** *"Cloud computing enhances efficiency by enabling real-time financial modeling and risk analysis, reducing capital expenditures."*

♦ **As an IT Consultant:** *"Cloud solutions provide scalable computing resources, essential for handling high-frequency trading and financial data analytics."*

♦ **As a Startup Founder:** *"Cloud computing minimizes infrastructure costs, allowing startups to scale their operations affordably without heavy upfront investments."*

Each response **maintains accuracy but shifts focus** based on the designated role.

3. When to Use Role-Based Prompting

Role-based prompting is useful in **a wide range of scenarios**, particularly when you need the AI to **adopt a specific perspective**.

a) *Business & Consulting*

When generating reports, strategies, or business analyses, role-based prompting can help tailor responses to **professional insights**.

Example   **Prompt:**
"You are a management consultant. Provide a strategic plan for a retail business looking to expand into e-commerce, considering supply chain logistics, digital marketing, and customer retention."

This ensures **the response reflects a consultant's strategic approach**, rather than a general list of e-commerce tips.

b) *Software Development & Technical Fields*

Developers and IT professionals can use role-based prompting to **enhance code quality, debugging, and technical explanations**.

Example **Prompt:**
"You are a senior Python developer. Write an optimized function to process large datasets efficiently, ensuring memory management and performance scalability."

This results in **a more structured and optimized solution** than a generic coding answer.

c) *Marketing & Content Creation*

Marketers can refine AI-generated content by specifying **a particular marketing role** to align responses with industry best practices.

Example **Prompt:**
"You are a digital marketing strategist. Write a LinkedIn ad targeting B2B SaaS companies, emphasizing cost savings and operational efficiency."

This helps **focus the content on a professional audience and strategic messaging.**

d) *Customer Support & Training*

Customer service and HR professionals can use role-based prompting to create **effective responses for training, support documentation, and internal communication**.

Example **Prompt:**
"You are a customer service manager. Draft a response to a customer complaint about delayed shipping, ensuring a professional and empathetic tone."

This guarantees the response **maintains brand professionalism and resolves the issue tactfully**.

4. How to Effectively Apply Role-Based Prompting

To maximize the effectiveness of role-based prompting, follow these **best practices**:

Step 1: *Clearly Define the Role*

Ensure the AI understands its assigned perspective by being **explicit about the role**.

✅ **Example:**
"You are a cybersecurity expert specializing in cloud security. Explain the best practices for preventing data breaches in a corporate environment."

This **narrows the AI's focus** to security concerns rather than general cloud computing benefits.

Step 2: *Specify the Audience*

Indicating **who the response is intended for** helps tailor the explanation.

✅ **Example:**
"You are a financial analyst. Explain inflation trends in simple terms for a non-financial audience."

This prompts Copilot to use **layman's terms instead of industry jargon**.

Step 3: *Provide Context & Constraints*

Adding **specific details** makes AI responses more relevant.

✅ **Example:**
"You are a medical researcher. Summarize the latest findings on AI in healthcare in under 300 words."

This ensures **concise, informative content** rather than an overly broad discussion.

Step 4: *Iterate & Refine*

If the initial response isn't perfect, refine the prompt by adjusting the role or adding more constraints.

🔄 **Follow-Up Prompt:**
"Make the explanation more persuasive, as if you were pitching to investors."

This adjusts the **tone and focus** for the intended audience.

5. Examples of Role-Based Prompting in Action

Scenario 1: Writing a Legal Document

✕ **Generic Prompt:**
"Write an explanation of intellectual property rights."

✓ **Role-Based Prompt:**
"You are an intellectual property attorney. Draft a legal guide on copyright, trademark, and patent protections for startup founders."

Scenario 2: Generating a Business Strategy

✕ **Generic Prompt:**
"How can a company improve customer loyalty?"

✓ **Role-Based Prompt:**
"You are a CRM strategist. Outline a customer retention plan for an online subscription service, focusing on engagement, personalization, and loyalty programs."

Scenario 3: Enhancing Technical Support

✕ **Generic Prompt:**
"Explain how to fix a slow internet connection."

✓ **Role-Based Prompt:**
"You are an IT help desk technician. Provide a troubleshooting guide for a customer experiencing slow Wi-Fi, including common causes and step-by-step solutions."

6. Conclusion: Enhancing AI Effectiveness with Role-Based Prompting

By **assigning roles to AI models like Microsoft Copilot**, users can generate **more relevant, accurate, and context-specific responses** tailored to different tasks and industries. **Role-based prompting ensures that AI understands the expectations, tone, and level of expertise needed for a given response.**

Key Takeaways:

✓ **Role-based prompts improve accuracy and depth** by aligning AI responses with professional   expertise.

✓ **They enhance tone, style, and clarity** to match different audiences and use cases.

✓ **They work across multiple fields**, including business, marketing, technical support,   legal   writing,   and   more.

✓ **Iterating on role-based prompts refines responses further**, ensuring high-quality AI assistance.

By leveraging **role-based prompting effectively**, users can turn **Microsoft Copilot into a powerful, specialized assistant** that delivers expert-level insights, tailored guidance, and high-value responses across a wide range of applications. 🚀

Fine-Tuning Prompts for Industry-Specific Needs

Microsoft Copilot is a powerful AI assistant that can provide useful insights across various industries. However, for **maximum accuracy, relevance, and value**, it is essential to fine-tune prompts based on **industry-specific needs**. Generic prompts often yield **broad, surface-level answers**, while well-crafted industry-focused prompts result in **more precise and actionable insights**.

Fine-tuning   prompts   involves   incorporating   **domain-specific terminology, constraints, and real-world context** to guide Copilot toward producing **high-quality, specialized responses**. In this article, we will explore **why industry-specific prompts matter, how to structure them effectively, and examples from different sectors**.

1. Why Industry-Specific Prompts Matter

AI models like Copilot are trained on **vast amounts of general knowledge**, but **they do not automatically prioritize industry-specific details** unless explicitly guided. Fine-tuned prompts:

✅ **Enhance Accuracy** – Ensure Copilot generates responses that align with industry best   practices.

✅ **Improve Contextual Understanding** – Avoid vague, generic answers by incorporating   real-world   industry   terminology.

☑ **Increase Relevance** – Help AI produce information that is directly useful to professionals   in   that   field.

☑ **Boost Efficiency** – Minimize time spent revising or reformatting AI-generated outputs.

For example, consider a **healthcare-related prompt**:

✗   **Generic**   **Prompt:**
"What are best practices for patient care?"

✓   **Industry-Specific**   **Prompt:**
"You are a hospital administrator specializing in patient experience. Outline a strategy for improving patient satisfaction in emergency departments, considering wait times, staff communication, and pain management."

The fine-tuned prompt **directs Copilot toward specific, actionable advice relevant to healthcare settings.**

2. Key Strategies for Fine-Tuning Prompts by Industry

a) *Use Industry Terminology & Jargon*

Each industry has its own **specialized vocabulary**. Including these terms helps Copilot provide **more professional, context-aware responses**.

Example   **(Finance):**
"Explain the implications of the Federal Reserve's interest rate hikes on corporate bond yields and investment strategies."

This prompt is **industry-specific**, encouraging a response tailored to financial professionals rather than a general audience.

b) *Define the Audience & Purpose*

A response for **entry-level professionals** should be different from one meant for **C-suite executives or researchers**. Clearly specifying the **target audience and purpose** improves the relevance of AI-generated content.

Example (Technology – Cybersecurity):
"You are a cybersecurity consultant advising a Fortune 500 company. Draft a security policy for remote employees, focusing on endpoint protection and data encryption."

This ensures Copilot generates a **detailed, business-oriented** response instead of a **generic cybersecurity guide**.

c) *Set Constraints & Formatting Preferences*

For industries where structure matters (e.g., legal, engineering, journalism), setting formatting guidelines helps Copilot deliver **well-organized, compliant outputs**.

Example (Legal Writing):
"Draft a privacy policy for a fintech mobile app. Structure it into sections including data collection, user rights, third-party sharing, and GDPR compliance."

This prompt **ensures Copilot follows a structured format**, improving the usability of the response.

d) *Reference Real-World Scenarios or Trends*

Adding industry-specific **case studies, regulations, or current trends** leads to more insightful, up-to-date AI-generated content.

Example (Marketing):
"Analyze how AI-driven personalization is impacting e-commerce conversion rates, referencing recent trends from Shopify and Amazon."

By instructing Copilot to **incorporate industry developments**, the response becomes **more relevant and data driven**.

3. Industry-Specific Prompt Examples

Fine-tuning prompts can be applied across numerous industries, from **healthcare and finance** to **marketing and engineering**. Below are examples of **how tailored prompts improve AI-generated outputs**.

a) Healthcare & Medicine

✖ **Generic** **Prompt:**
"What are the benefits of telemedicine?"

✔ **Fine-Tuned** **Prompt:**
"You are a healthcare consultant advising a rural hospital network. Assess the impact of telemedicine on patient accessibility, insurance reimbursement challenges, and physician workload."

This version **focuses on a specific healthcare setting and critical industry concerns**.

b) Financial Services & Banking

✖ **Generic** **Prompt:**
"What are some good investment strategies?"

✔ **Fine-Tuned** **Prompt:**
"You are a portfolio manager at an investment firm. Compare the risk-adjusted returns of dividend stocks versus corporate bonds in a high-inflation environment."

This ensures Copilot **provides a professional, data-driven response relevant to investors**.

c) Software Development & AI Engineering

✖ **Generic** **Prompt:**
"How can we improve software performance?"

✔ **Fine-Tuned** **Prompt:**
"You are a senior DevOps engineer optimizing a cloud-based SaaS platform. Outline strategies to reduce latency and improve system reliability, considering auto-scaling and database indexing."

This **guides Copilot to generate a response aligned with modern DevOps challenges.**

d) Manufacturing & Supply Chain

✘ **Generic** **Prompt:**
"What are the challenges in supply chain management?"

✓ **Fine-Tuned** **Prompt:**
"You are a logistics manager for an international retail company. Identify key challenges in global supply chains post-pandemic and suggest mitigation strategies, focusing on supplier diversification and inventory forecasting."

Now, the response will be **specific to real-world logistics concerns** rather than generic supply chain issues.

e) Journalism & Media

✘ **Generic** **Prompt:**
"Write a news report about climate change."

✓ **Fine-Tuned** **Prompt:**
"You are a science journalist writing for a national newspaper. Draft a 500-word article summarizing the latest IPCC report findings on climate change's economic impact, citing expert opinions."

This ensures **accuracy, proper structure, and journalistic integrity**.

4. Fine-Tuning Prompts for Cross-Industry Applications

Some prompts may need **cross-industry fine-tuning**, depending on the use case. Consider **AI ethics**, where different sectors have unique concerns:

AI in Healthcare vs. AI in Finance

✦ **Healthcare** **Prompt:**
"You are an AI ethicist advising a hospital. Evaluate the ethical concerns of using AI for patient diagnostics, including bias and privacy risks."

"You are a regulatory expert assessing AI-driven stock trading algorithms. Discuss compliance risks and SEC regulations regarding algorithmic trading transparency."

Though both prompts address AI ethics, they **focus on industry-specific concerns**, making them more useful.

5. Conclusion: Why Fine-Tuning Prompts Is Essential for Industry-Specific AI Use

Fine-tuning prompts **transforms Microsoft Copilot from a general AI assistant into an industry-specialized tool** that delivers highly relevant, insightful, and actionable content. **By incorporating domain-specific language, structuring responses for professional use, and referencing real-world challenges, AI-generated outputs become significantly more valuable.**

Key Takeaways:

✓ **Industry-specific prompts lead to more relevant, expert-level responses.**
✓ **Defining the audience and purpose helps tailor AI outputs.**
✓ **Using structured formatting improves readability and compliance in regulated**   **industries.**
✓ **Incorporating real-world scenarios ensures up-to-date, practical insights.**

By mastering industry-specific prompt engineering, businesses and professionals can **unlock the full potential of Microsoft Copilot**, making it a **true AI-powered industry assistant rather than just a text generator.** 🚀

VII. Case Studies and Real-World Applications

Examples of Effective Prompt Engineering in Different Industries

Prompt engineering plays a crucial role in ensuring that **Microsoft Copilot** and other AI-powered tools generate **highly relevant, accurate, and actionable responses** tailored to different professional fields. Each industry has unique challenges, terminology, and requirements, meaning **a well-crafted prompt** can significantly impact the quality of AI-generated outputs.

In this article, we will explore **real-world examples of effective prompt engineering across various industries**, including healthcare, finance, marketing, legal, education, and more. By structuring prompts correctly and incorporating **specific industry details, formatting preferences, and contextual nuances**, professionals can **maximize AI's value in their workflows**.

1. Healthcare & Medical Research

Scenario 1: Medical Diagnosis Support

✖ **Generic Prompt:**
"What are the symptoms of diabetes?"

✓ **Effective Prompt:**
"You are an endocrinologist. Explain the early warning signs of Type 2 diabetes, differentiating between mild, moderate, and severe cases. Keep the explanation patient-friendly and under 300 words."

- ◆ **Why It Works:**

  - Specifies **a professional role (endocrinologist)** to guide AI toward **expert-level** medical advice.
  - Clarifies the **depth of response** by asking for different **severity levels**.
  - Ensures **patient-friendly language** for accessibility.

Scenario 2: Medical Research Analysis

✗ **Generic** **Prompt:**
"Summarize research on AI in healthcare."

✓ **Effective** **Prompt:**
"You are a medical researcher specializing in AI applications in healthcare. Summarize the latest studies (post-2022) on AI-assisted diagnostics, highlighting accuracy rates, ethical concerns, and regulatory challenges. Structure the response in bullet points for easy readability."

◆ **Why It Works:**

- Narrows focus to **recent studies** for up-to-date insights.
- Mentions **key discussion areas** (accuracy, ethics, regulations).
- Requests **bullet points** for better readability.

. Finance & Banking

Scenario 1: Investment Strategies

✗ **Generic** **Prompt:**
"Give me investment advice."

✓ **Effective** **Prompt:**
"You are a financial advisor specializing in portfolio management. Compare the risk and return potential of dividend stocks, corporate bonds, and real estate investment trusts (REITs) in a high-inflation environment. Use data-driven insights."

◆ **Why It Works:**

- **Specifies** a **financial role** to focus the AI's expertise.
- Defines **asset classes** (stocks, bonds, REITs) to keep the response relevant.
- Requests **a data-driven approach**, avoiding vague suggestions.

Scenario 2: Regulatory Compliance

✗ **Generic** **Prompt:**
"Explain financial regulations."

✓ **Effective** **Prompt:**
"You are a compliance officer at a multinational bank. Summarize key changes in SEC

regulations affecting cryptocurrency trading in 2024, including penalties for non-compliance."

- ◆ **Why It Works:**

  - Assigns **a professional role (compliance officer)** for **precise regulatory guidance**.
  - Focuses on **current regulations (2024)** rather than outdated information.
  - Includes **penalties**, making it actionable for businesses.

3. Marketing & Advertising

Scenario 1: Social Media Strategy

✖ **Generic** **Prompt:**
"How do I grow my brand on Instagram?"

✓ **Effective** **Prompt:**
"You are a social media strategist for a DTC (direct-to-consumer) skincare brand. Develop a six-month Instagram marketing plan focused on influencer partnerships, UGC (user-generated content), and paid ad campaigns. Provide a month-by-month breakdown."

- ◆ **Why It Works:**

  - **Targets a specific industry (skincare)** rather than general social media advice.
  - Includes **key strategies** (influencer marketing, UGC, paid ads).
  - Requests **a structured plan (month-by-month)** for practical implementation.

Scenario 2: Copywriting for a Product Launch

✖ **Generic** **Prompt:**
"Write an ad for a new smartwatch."

✓ **Effective** **Prompt:**
"You are a copywriter at a tech company launching a premium smartwatch. Write a compelling Facebook ad emphasizing its AI-powered health tracking, 7-day battery life, and water-resistant design. Keep it under 150 words with a strong CTA (call to action)."

- ◆ **Why It Works:**

  - Specifies **ad platform (Facebook)** for the right format.

- Highlights **key product features** for a focused message.
- Sets a **word limit (150 words)** to keep it concise.

4. Legal & Compliance

Scenario 1: Contract Drafting

✕   **Generic**   **Prompt:**
"Write a business contract."

✓   **Effective**   **Prompt:**
"You are a corporate attorney drafting a partnership agreement for a tech startup. Include sections on revenue sharing, intellectual property ownership, dispute resolution, and contract termination. Ensure compliance with U.S. business laws."

◆ **Why It Works:**

- Defines **contract type** (partnership agreement).
- Lists **critical sections** to include.
- Specifies **U.S. legal compliance** for jurisdictional accuracy.

Scenario 2: Employment Law Advice

✕   **Generic**   **Prompt:**
"Explain employee rights."

✓   **Effective**   **Prompt:**
"You are an employment lawyer. Summarize employee rights related to remote work, overtime pay, and discrimination in the workplace under U.S. labor laws. Provide citations where possible."

◆ **Why It Works:**

- Specifies **employee rights in a modern work environment (remote work, overtime, discrimination).**
- Requests **citations** to ensure factual accuracy.

5. Education & E-Learning

Scenario 1: Lesson Plan Development

✕ **Generic** **Prompt:**
"Create a lesson plan on world history."

✓ **Effective** **Prompt:**
"You are a high school history teacher preparing a lesson on the causes and impacts of World War II. Design a 60-minute interactive lesson plan, including discussion topics, multimedia resources, and a short quiz."

◆ **Why It Works:**

- Specifies **subject focus (WWII causes & impacts)**.
- Requests **interactive elements** for student engagement.
- Includes **a quiz** to measure comprehension.

Scenario 2: Personalized Learning Recommendations

✕ **Generic** **Prompt:**
"Suggest study techniques."

✓ **Effective** **Prompt:**
"You are an academic coach helping a college student prepare for a physics exam. Suggest effective study techniques, including active recall, spaced repetition, and problem-solving exercises, tailored for STEM subjects."

◆ **Why It Works:**

- Focuses on **physics/STEM subjects** rather than generic study habits.
- Incorporates **proven learning strategies** like active recall.

Conclusion: Why Industry-Specific Prompt Engineering Matters

Effective prompt engineering **transforms AI responses** from **generic to highly specialized and valuable**. By specifying **roles, industry context, formatting preferences, and constraints**, professionals can make **Microsoft Copilot a powerful assistant tailored to their specific needs**.

Key Takeaways:

✓ **Use industry-specific terminology** to ensure Copilot provides expert-level responses.

✓ **Define a clear role or persona** to match AI-generated content with professional expectations.

✓ **Set formatting or structural preferences** (e.g., bullet points, word limits) for clarity.

✓ **Request specific insights or trends** to get up-to-date, data-driven responses.

By applying these strategies across **healthcare, finance, marketing, legal, education, and beyond**, professionals can leverage **AI-driven efficiency without compromising accuracy or relevance**. 🚀

Success Stories of Businesses Leveraging Microsoft Copilot Efficiently

Microsoft Copilot has rapidly transformed the way businesses operate, enhancing productivity, improving decision-making, and streamlining workflows across various industries. Companies that have strategically integrated Copilot into their processes have reported **significant efficiency gains, reduced workloads, and improved output quality**. This article highlights **real-world success stories** of businesses that have effectively leveraged Microsoft Copilot, showcasing its impact on **finance, healthcare, marketing, legal, software development, and education**.

1.Financial Services: Automating Reports and Enhancing Insights

Company: Global Investment Firm

A leading **investment management company** struggled with manually generating **financial reports, market analysis, and risk assessments**, which consumed excessive time and resources. By integrating **Microsoft Copilot into their Microsoft 365 ecosystem**, they automated:

- ✅ **Quarterly financial reports**, reducing report generation time by 70%.
- ✅ **Market trend analysis**, using AI-powered summaries and comparisons.
- ✅ **Risk assessment modeling**, leveraging Copilot to analyze investment risks.

Before Copilot, **analysts spent hours manually summarizing financial reports**. Now, **with a well-structured prompt**, Copilot **instantly extracts key insights from massive datasets**, allowing analysts to focus on strategic decision-making.

📌 **Example Prompt Used:**
"You are a financial analyst summarizing the last quarter's investment performance. Identify key trends in global equity markets, emerging risks, and high-performing sectors. Structure insights in a 300-word executive summary."

Impact:

The firm saw **a 60% reduction in reporting workload**, allowing analysts to **focus on high-value investment strategies** instead of tedious data processing.

2.Healthcare: Enhancing Documentation & Patient Communication

Company: Large Hospital Network

Hospitals generate massive amounts of **clinical documentation**, and doctors spend **nearly a third of their time on paperwork** instead of patient care. A major **hospital network integrated Microsoft Copilot** to:

- ✅ **Auto-generate patient discharge summaries** based on doctor's notes.
- ✅ **Draft patient-friendly explanations** of complex medical conditions.
- ✅ **Assist in medical research documentation** for faster clinical trials.

Before using Copilot, physicians manually wrote discharge summaries, taking **20-30 minutes per patient**. With Copilot, summaries are generated in **seconds**, requiring only **quick edits** for personalization.

📌 **Example Prompt Used:**
"You are a medical assistant summarizing a doctor's notes for a patient discharge

summary. Ensure the language is simple and accessible, and include key recovery guidelines and follow-up recommendations."

Impact:

The hospital reported **a 50% reduction in documentation time**, allowing doctors to **see more patients daily** while ensuring **higher accuracy in medical records**.

3. Marketing & Advertising: Boosting Content Creation Efficiency

Company: E-Commerce Retailer

A fast-growing **online fashion retailer** struggled with **content production for social media, product descriptions, and email campaigns**. By adopting **Copilot for content creation**, they:

- ☑ **Generated product descriptions** 80% faster, ensuring SEO optimization.
- ☑ **Created personalized email campaigns** using AI-driven audience segmentation.
- ☑ **Drafted engaging social media posts**, increasing brand engagement.

Before Copilot, the team manually wrote each product description, taking **5-7 minutes per product**. With Copilot, they now generate descriptions in **under a minute**, allowing copywriters to **focus on creativity and refinement rather than repetitive tasks**.

📌 **Example Prompt Used:**
"You are a marketing copywriter for an e-commerce fashion brand. Write a compelling product description for a new eco-friendly sneaker, emphasizing sustainability, comfort, and style. Keep it under 100 words and SEO-friendly."

Impact:

The company **tripled its content output** and saw **a 35% increase in customer engagement** due to faster, high-quality content production.

4. Legal Services: Streamlining Contract Review and Compliance

Company: Corporate Law Firm

A multinational **law firm** dealing with **large volumes of contracts and compliance documents** struggled with **time-consuming manual reviews**. By integrating Copilot, they:

- ✅ **Automated contract analysis**, highlighting key clauses and risks.
- ✅ **Generated compliance summaries** for regulatory changes.
- ✅ **Drafted legal documents** faster, reducing attorney workload.

Before Copilot, junior lawyers spent **several hours manually reviewing contracts**. Now, Copilot processes **hundreds of pages within minutes**, flagging **critical clauses for review**.

📌 **Example Prompt Used:**
"You are a legal analyst reviewing a vendor contract. Identify clauses related to liability, termination rights, and indemnification. Summarize potential risks in bullet points."

Impact:

The firm reported **a 40% faster contract review process**, allowing lawyers to **focus on high-value legal analysis rather than repetitive document scanning**.

5. Software Development: Accelerating Coding and Debugging

Company: SaaS Tech Startup

A **SaaS (Software as a Service) company** struggled with **slow development cycles and debugging challenges**. By integrating **GitHub Copilot**, they:

- ✅ **Automated repetitive code writing**, reducing errors and time spent.
- ✅ **Improved debugging efficiency**, as Copilot suggested optimized solutions.
- ✅ **Enhanced documentation**, with AI-generated inline comments.

Before Copilot, junior developers took **hours troubleshooting bugs**. Now, Copilot **suggests real-time code fixes**, dramatically reducing development bottlenecks.

"You are a senior software engineer working on a Python-based SaaS platform. Suggest an optimized function to handle user authentication, ensuring security best practices and efficiency."

Impact:

The company saw **a 50% reduction in coding time** and faster software releases, allowing them to **bring new features to market ahead of competitors**.

6. Education & E-Learning: Enhancing Personalized Learning

Company: Online Learning Platform

An **edtech company** offering **personalized tutoring** faced challenges in **scaling lesson plans and generating educational materials**. With Copilot, they:

- ☑ **Generated lesson plans tailored to different learning styles.**
- ☑ **Created personalized study guides for students.**
- ☑ **Developed AI-powered quiz questions** based on student progress.

Before Copilot, **curriculum designers manually created lesson plans**, consuming **significant time**. Now, Copilot generates **structured lesson plans** within minutes, which teachers refine and customize.

📌 **Example Prompt Used:**
"You are an educational consultant designing a physics lesson for high school students. Create a 45-minute lesson plan covering Newton's Laws, including an interactive experiment and discussion questions."

Impact:

The company saw a **40% increase in course material production efficiency**, allowing **faster course rollouts and more personalized student engagement**.

Conclusion: The Power of Copilot in Business Success

These real-world success stories highlight **how businesses across multiple industries** have leveraged **Microsoft Copilot to streamline workflows, enhance productivity, and improve quality**. Whether in **finance, healthcare, marketing, legal, software development, or education**, organizations that strategically integrate Copilot achieve **tangible time savings, cost reductions, and better decision-making.**

Key Takeaways:

✓ **Financial firms** use Copilot for **faster reporting and market insights**.

✓ **Hospitals** leverage Copilot to **reduce medical documentation workloads**.

✓ **Marketing teams** improve **content creation and engagement** with AI-driven copywriting.

✓ **Law firms** streamline **contract review and compliance analysis**.

✓ **Developers** write **cleaner, more efficient code** using AI assistance.

✓ **Educators** scale **lesson planning and personalized learning materials**.

By harnessing **AI-powered Copilot capabilities**, businesses are **transforming their operations, increasing efficiency, and staying ahead of the competition** in today's digital economy. 🚀

VIII. Conclusion and Next Steps

Recap of Key Strategies for Effective Microsoft Copilot Prompt Engineering

Mastering Microsoft Copilot's prompt engineering techniques is crucial for maximizing its efficiency, accuracy, and overall usefulness. Throughout this guide, we have explored numerous strategies that help refine how users interact with Copilot to achieve optimal responses. Below is a **comprehensive recap** of the key strategies that can elevate your Copilot experience, whether you're using it for **business documents, coding, content creation, or data analysis.**

1. Understanding the Importance of Prompt Engineering

Prompt engineering is the foundation of using AI tools like Microsoft Copilot effectively. Without clear, well-structured prompts, **responses can be vague, irrelevant, or inaccurate**. Recognizing that AI models rely entirely on the inputs provided ensures that users take an **intentional approach to crafting prompts** that guide Copilot toward the desired outcome.

To achieve the best results, users should focus on:

- **Clarity** – Ensuring the request is unambiguous.
- **Context** – Providing relevant background information.
- **Constraints** – Setting word limits, formatting, or style guidelines.

By carefully structuring prompts, users can ensure **concise, well-targeted outputs** that meet their needs.

2. Structuring Prompts for Optimal Responses

One of the most effective ways to improve Copilot's outputs is by **structuring prompts properly**. A well-structured prompt:

- **Begins with clear intent** (e.g., "Summarize this report...").
- **Provides context** (e.g., "For a marketing team working on a campaign...").
- **Includes format guidance** (e.g., "In bullet points, under 200 words...").

📌 **Example of an unstructured vs. structured prompt:**

❌ *"Tell me about climate change."* (Too broad and vague)
✅ *"Summarize the main causes of climate change in 100 words, focusing on human impact and natural contributors. Present the response as bullet points."* (Clear, contextual, and structured)

When prompts are **concise yet detailed**, Copilot can **generate highly relevant responses with minimal edits needed**.

3. Aligning Prompts with Specific Tasks

Microsoft Copilot is used across various industries and tasks, from **business writing to coding**. Therefore, crafting prompts that **align with specific objectives** helps Copilot deliver more tailored results.

For example, in **coding**, Copilot can assist with debugging, code generation, and optimization:

📌 **Example:** *"Generate a Python function that sorts a list of numbers using quicksort. Include inline comments explaining each step."*

In **business communication**, prompts should be tailored to professional needs:

📌 **Example:** *"Draft a formal email apologizing for a product delay, offering a 10% discount as compensation."*

By tailoring the prompt to the **specific task**, users can **eliminate ambiguity and receive precise results.**

4. Using Background Information to Refine Responses

AI models **do not inherently understand nuanced requests** unless background information is provided. Adding context can significantly improve response quality, especially in specialized fields.

📌 **Example:** Instead of: *"Write a business proposal,"* Use: *"Write a business proposal for a small startup seeking investors for an AI-powered customer service chatbot. Highlight potential market growth and revenue projections."*

Providing **industry, audience, or purpose-specific information** helps Copilot **generate a more targeted and refined response.**

5. Leveraging Constraints Like Word Limits, Styles, and Formats

Setting **clear constraints** in a prompt prevents AI from generating overly verbose or unfocused responses. Constraints can include:

- **Word limits** (*"Summarize this in 150 words."*)
- **Tone/style guidelines** (*"Write in a formal and persuasive tone."*)
- **Output format** (*"List key takeaways in a numbered format."*)

📌 **Example:**

❌ *"Explain Newton's laws."* (Too broad)

✅ *"Summarize Newton's three laws of motion in simple language, in 100 words or less, and format them as bullet points."* (Well-structured and constrained)

Using constraints ensures **concise, structured, and useful responses.**

6. Breaking Down Multi-Step Requests

If a task involves **multiple steps**, asking Copilot to handle everything in one long prompt may lead to **confusing or incomplete answers**. Instead, breaking requests into **smaller, sequential prompts** helps maintain accuracy.

📌 **Example of a complex request:**

❌ *"Write a marketing email and a landing page script for a new product launch."* (Too broad—Copilot may not handle both equally well.)

✅ **Breaking it down into steps:**

1️⃣ *"Write a compelling marketing email introducing our new smart fitness tracker. Focus on its health benefits and exclusive launch discount."*

2️⃣ *"Now create a landing page script for the same product, emphasizing real customer testimonials and a strong call to action."*

By using sequential prompts, **each output is more focused and polished**.

7. Using Chain-of-Thought and Role-Based Prompting

For more complex reasoning tasks, **chain-of-thought prompting** helps Copilot break down problems step by step.

📌 **Example:**

"Explain how AI chatbots improve customer service. Start with their impact on response

time, then discuss personalization, and finally, cost-effectiveness. Structure as three short paragraphs."

Role-based prompting also refines results by **assigning Copilot a perspective**:
✦ **Example:** *"You are a senior financial advisor. Explain cryptocurrency risks to a beginner investor."*

These methods help **ensure logical flow and well-structured insights.**

8. Analyzing and Iterating on Responses

No AI model provides **perfect answers on the first try**. Reviewing and refining Copilot's responses ensures **accuracy, clarity, and alignment with user needs**.

If a response is **too generic**, users can prompt:
✦ *"Make this explanation more detailed with examples."*

If a response is **too long**, they can refine it with:
✦ *"Summarize this in 3 key points."*

Iteration is key to **harnessing Copilot's full potential** in **delivering high-quality, tailored responses.**

Conclusion: Mastering Copilot Through Strategic Prompting

By applying these strategies, users can **maximize Microsoft Copilot's efficiency and accuracy** across different domains. Key takeaways include:

✓ **Write clear, structured prompts** to guide Copilot effectively.
✓ **Provide context** to refine responses and improve relevance.
✓ **Use constraints** like word limits and formatting for better readability.
✓ **Break down complex requests** into smaller, sequential steps.

✓ **Apply role-based and chain-of-thought prompting** for advanced reasoning.

✓ **Iterate and refine responses** to achieve the best results.

With **well-crafted prompts**, Copilot transforms from a generic AI assistant into a **powerful tool tailored to individual needs**, enhancing productivity and ensuring high-quality outputs. 🚀

Encouragement to Experiment and Refine Prompts

Using Microsoft Copilot effectively is not just about following rigid rules—it's about **experimenting, refining, and adapting** prompts to get the best possible responses. AI models, including Copilot, thrive on **iterative input**, meaning that small tweaks to a prompt can significantly improve the output. By adopting a mindset of **curiosity and flexibility**, users can unlock Copilot's full potential for generating high-quality responses.

The Importance of Experimentation

When first using Copilot, some responses may not be perfect. Instead of assuming the AI is limited, consider **reworking the prompt** in different ways. A single question or request can be framed in multiple formats, and each variation might yield **different levels of depth, clarity, or specificity** in the response.

For example, a user asking for a **summary of an article** might start with:
❌ *"Summarize this article."* (Too vague)
✅ *"Summarize this article in 100 words, focusing on key findings and practical applications."* (More specific)

By **testing multiple versions of a prompt**, users can identify what works best for their needs and develop a deeper understanding of how Copilot interprets requests.

Refining Prompts for Better Precision

The **first attempt** at a prompt might produce a response that is **too general, too detailed, or slightly off-topic**. Instead of settling for that result, **iterating** on the prompt can improve accuracy.

For instance, if a marketing professional asks Copilot to write an **email campaign** but finds the output too formal, they might adjust the wording:

❌ *"Write an email promoting our new software."* (Unclear tone)
✅ *"Write a casual, engaging email promoting our new project management software to startup founders. Highlight ease of use and affordability."* (Better-targeted)

Each small change—whether in **tone, structure, or detail level**—helps refine Copilot's responses to better fit the intended purpose.

The Power of Feedback Loops

Experimentation is most effective when paired with **a feedback loop**. After generating an initial response, users should review it and ask:

- **Does this answer my question fully?**
- **Is the tone and detail level appropriate?**
- **Are there any missing elements that I need to clarify?**

If the response is **not quite right**, the user can rephrase the request to **steer Copilot in the right direction**. Instead of manually fixing the response, an improved prompt can help Copilot refine it further.

📌 **Example of a feedback loop in action:**
1️⃣ *First prompt: "Generate a business proposal for a new fitness app."*
2️⃣ *Response:* Too general, lacking key details.
3️⃣ *Refined prompt: "Generate a business proposal for a subscription-based fitness app focused on home workouts. Include market analysis, revenue model, and competitive advantages."*
4️⃣ *Response:* Now more aligned with expectations.

Each round of feedback brings the response **closer to the ideal result**.

Encouraging Creativity in Prompting

Some of the best results with Copilot come from **thinking outside the box** and exploring **unconventional prompting techniques**.

For instance, instead of just asking for a **generic blog post**, users can **infuse creativity into their prompts**:

"Write a blog post about time management as if it were a conversation between a productivity coach and a procrastinator."

By framing requests in unique ways, users can unlock **more engaging, diverse, and dynamic responses** from Copilot.

Embracing a Trial-and-Error Approach

Just like learning any new tool, becoming skilled at using Copilot requires **trial and error**. Users should not be discouraged by imperfect responses but should instead view them as **opportunities to refine their approach**.

Key steps for an **effective trial-and-error process** include:
✓ **Starting with a basic prompt and analyzing the response.**
✓ **Making small changes to improve clarity and specificity.**
✓ **Testing different formats, such as bullet points, numbered lists, or narratives.**
✓ **Observing how changes affect Copilot's output and adjusting accordingly.**

With time, users **develop an intuitive sense** of how to craft prompts that consistently yield **high-quality, relevant results**.

Final Encouragement: Keep Exploring and Refining

Using Microsoft Copilot is an ongoing journey of **discovery and improvement**. Every user—whether a business professional, developer, content creator, or researcher—can enhance their experience by **continuously testing new approaches** and **learning from past interactions**.

✓ **Be patient**—great results often come after a few iterations.
✓ **Be creative**—try different angles and formats for prompts.
✓ **Be analytical**—review responses and refine prompts accordingly.

By actively experimenting with prompt engineering, users **empower themselves** to extract **maximum value from Copilot**, transforming it from a simple assistant into a **powerful productivity partner.** 🚀

Additional Resources for Deepening Copilot Expertise

Mastering Microsoft Copilot is an ongoing process that requires continuous learning, experimentation, and adaptation. While this guide has covered essential strategies for prompt engineering, there are **numerous additional resources** available to further refine your skills and **expand your understanding** of how to leverage Copilot effectively. Whether you're a developer, business professional, or content creator, these resources will help you stay ahead of the curve and maximize Copilot's potential.

1. Microsoft's Official Documentation and Training

Microsoft provides **comprehensive documentation** on Copilot, including guides, FAQs, and best practices tailored to different versions, such as **Microsoft 365 Copilot, GitHub Copilot, and Copilot for Azure**. These resources are invaluable for understanding **updates, new features, and troubleshooting common issues**.

📌 **Where to start:**

- **Microsoft Learn** – Offers free, structured training modules on using AI in Microsoft 365.
- **Microsoft Copilot Official Documentation** – Covers setup, use cases, and tips for refining AI-generated outputs.
- **Microsoft Tech Community** – A forum where users can discuss Copilot features and share insights.

By regularly checking Microsoft's official resources, users can **stay informed** about improvements and new functionalities that can enhance their workflow.

2. Online Courses and Tutorials

For users who prefer a **guided, hands-on learning experience**, online courses can be a great way to gain deeper insights into **Copilot's capabilities**. Platforms like **LinkedIn Learning, Coursera, and Udemy** offer specialized courses on **prompt engineering, AI-assisted productivity, and coding with GitHub Copilot**.

❖ Recommended courses:

- **"Mastering Prompt Engineering for AI Assistants"** (Coursera)
- **"Microsoft Copilot for Business: The Complete Guide"** (LinkedIn Learning)
- **"GitHub Copilot for Developers: AI-Powered Coding"** (Udemy)

These courses typically include **real-world examples, exercises, and assessments**, making them ideal for users looking to **apply Copilot effectively** in their industry or profession.

3. AI and Prompt Engineering Communities

Engaging with **AI-focused communities** is one of the best ways to **learn from other users, troubleshoot issues, and discover advanced techniques**. AI enthusiasts, developers, and business professionals regularly share their experiences, best practices, and creative ways to use Copilot in different contexts.

❖ Popular AI and Copilot communities:

- **Reddit r/ArtificialIntelligence** – Discussions on AI tools, including Copilot.
- **Microsoft Copilot Forum** – A hub for official announcements, updates, and user discussions.
- **GitHub Discussions (for GitHub Copilot users)** – A great resource for developers seeking coding-specific insights.

By actively participating in these communities, users can **gain fresh perspectives, find solutions to common challenges, and share their own experiences** with Copilot.

4. Experimenting with OpenAI's Research and AI Papers

Since Copilot is powered by **OpenAI's language models**, exploring OpenAI's official research papers and blog posts can provide **deeper insights into how AI models interpret and generate text**. While not required for general users, understanding **the principles of AI model behavior** can help advanced users fine-tune their prompts for maximum efficiency.

Recommended readings:

- **"GPT Models and How They Work"** (OpenAI Blog)
- **"AI Ethics and Responsible AI Use"** (Microsoft Research)
- **"Advancements in Natural Language Processing"** (AI research papers from top institutions)

These resources help users **understand Copilot's limitations, strengths, and the evolving nature of AI-assisted tools**.

5. YouTube Tutorials and AI Webinars

For those who prefer **visual learning**, YouTube is an excellent platform for **free, high-quality tutorials** on using Copilot effectively. Many AI experts and Microsoft MVPs (Most Valuable Professionals) publish step-by-step guides, advanced use cases, and troubleshooting tips for Copilot.

Popular YouTube channels for learning Copilot:

- **Microsoft Mechanics** – Covers AI advancements, including Copilot.
- **AI Explained** – Breaks down AI trends and how to apply them.
- **CodeWithHarry (for GitHub Copilot users)** – Offers coding tips and AI-assisted development strategies.

Additionally, **Microsoft frequently hosts live webinars** where users can engage with **Copilot engineers and AI specialists**, ask questions, and **watch real-time demonstrations of new features**.

6. Blogs and Case Studies on AI in Business

For business professionals looking to integrate Copilot into their workflows, case studies and business-oriented AI blogs provide **practical insights** into how organizations are successfully using Copilot to **increase efficiency and automate tasks**.

Great sources for AI and Copilot in business:

- **Harvard Business Review (HBR AI & Business Section)** – Covers AI's impact on productivity.
- **Microsoft AI Blog** – Shares success stories of businesses leveraging Copilot.
- **TechCrunch AI Reports** – Tracks industry trends and real-world AI implementations.

Reading **success stories and industry applications** can spark ideas for **new ways to utilize Copilot effectively**.

7. Hands-On Practice with Different Prompting Styles

Ultimately, **the best way to deepen expertise** with Copilot is through **consistent practice and experimentation**. By actively using different prompting techniques—such as **chain-of-thought prompting, role-based prompting, and structured input constraints**—users can **discover what works best for their unique needs**.

📌 **Tips for hands-on practice:**

- **Set daily or weekly challenges** (e.g., use Copilot to draft an email, generate a report, or debug a piece of code).
- **Compare Copilot's responses** by tweaking prompts slightly and noting differences in output.
- **Use Copilot across different applications** (Microsoft Word, Excel, Teams, GitHub, etc.) to explore its full capabilities.

By refining prompting strategies over time, users can **transform Copilot into a highly customized AI assistant** that consistently delivers **high-quality, task-specific outputs**.

Final Thoughts: Keep Learning and Stay Updated

AI tools like Microsoft Copilot are constantly evolving, with **new features, updates, and improvements** being released regularly. Staying engaged with **official Microsoft resources, AI research, and expert communities** ensures that users **keep pace with these advancements** and continue refining their skills.

✓ Explore Microsoft's documentation and learning hubs.

✓ Join AI communities and discussion forums.

✓ Take online courses and attend webinars.

✓ Experiment with different prompting techniques.

✓ Stay informed on AI trends through research and industry blogs.

By committing to **ongoing learning and exploration**, users can **fully harness the power of Copilot**, turning it into an indispensable tool for **enhancing productivity, creativity, and efficiency**. 🚀

Glossary of Terms for Microsoft Copilot and Prompt Engineering

Here is a comprehensive glossary of key terms and concepts related to **Microsoft Copilot**, **AI-assisted productivity**, and **prompt engineering**. This glossary will help deepen your understanding of the terminology often encountered when working with Copilot and other AI models.

AI (Artificial Intelligence)

The simulation of human intelligence in machines that are programmed to think, learn, and problem-solve. Copilot utilizes AI to assist users by generating text, performing tasks, and providing insights.

API (Application Programming Interface)

A set of protocols and tools for building software applications. In the context of Copilot, APIs are used to connect Copilot's AI model with other tools, such as Microsoft 365 or GitHub, enabling seamless interactions.

Chain-of-Thought Prompting

A method where prompts are structured in a sequence of logical steps to guide the AI toward more complex reasoning or problem-solving. This technique is especially useful for tasks requiring multi-step processes or complex analysis.

Contextualized Prompt

A prompt that includes relevant background information, details, or context to help the AI generate a more accurate, relevant, and specific response.

Copilot

An AI-powered assistant developed by Microsoft, integrated into applications like Microsoft 365 and GitHub, to assist users in performing tasks more efficiently, such as generating content, writing code, and answering questions.

Data Preprocessing

The process of preparing and organizing raw data to make it suitable for AI models. In prompt engineering, this can refer to structuring inputs in a way that enhances AI understanding and response quality.

Feedback Loop

A process where initial outputs or responses from AI are reviewed, and adjustments are made to the input prompt or parameters to improve subsequent responses. This iterative cycle of testing, feedback, and refinement is key to effective prompt engineering.

Fine-Tuning

The process of adjusting a pre-trained AI model's parameters to optimize performance for a specific task or domain. In prompt engineering, fine-tuning involves carefully adjusting prompts to achieve desired results more consistently.

GitHub Copilot

A version of Copilot that helps developers by suggesting code completions, debugging, and writing code in real-time, powered by AI models trained on publicly available coding data.

Iteration

The process of repeating a series of steps, making refinements or changes along the way, to improve results. In prompt engineering, iteration involves testing and modifying prompts to achieve better or more accurate AI responses.

Natural Language Processing (NLP)

A branch of AI focused on enabling machines to understand and interpret human language in a way that is useful. Copilot's effectiveness in generating responses is largely due to its NLP capabilities.

Non-Contextualized Prompt

A prompt that lacks essential background information, making it more difficult for the AI to generate precise, context-aware responses. Non-contextualized prompts are often too vague or broad.

Optimization

The process of making improvements or adjustments to an AI model, system, or prompt to make it perform better, such as generating more accurate responses or reducing processing time.

Prompt

The input provided to an AI model, instructing it to perform a task or generate a response. Effective prompts are clear, specific, and well-structured to ensure optimal results.

Prompt Engineering

The practice of crafting and refining prompts to guide AI models in generating responses that are useful, accurate, and aligned with the user's goals. It involves understanding how AI interprets input and structuring prompts accordingly.

Prompt Structure

The way a prompt is organized, including its length, complexity, and clarity. Effective prompt structure plays a critical role in determining the quality and relevance of the AI-generated response.

Role-Based Prompting

A technique where the user assigns a specific role or persona to the AI in the prompt, helping guide the model's tone, style, or behavior. For example, asking the AI to "act as a marketing expert" to generate specialized content.

Sequential Prompts

A technique where multiple prompts are used in sequence, with each prompt building on the previous one. This is often used for complex tasks that require several steps or stages of input.

Specificity

The level of detail and clarity in a prompt. A more specific prompt provides clearer instructions, reducing ambiguity and increasing the chances of receiving a relevant response.

Syntax

The structure and rules governing how language is used in prompts. Proper syntax helps ensure that the AI correctly interprets the prompt and provides the desired output.

Test Case

A scenario or example used to evaluate how effectively an AI model handles a particular prompt. Test cases help users identify areas where their prompts need refinement to achieve the best results.

Tone

The style or emotional quality of the language used in a prompt. Tone is critical for AI responses in certain tasks, such as crafting emails or marketing content, where a specific emotional appeal or formality level is required.

User Intent

The goal or purpose behind the prompt, such as generating text, solving a problem, or answering a question. Understanding user intent helps in crafting more effective and efficient prompts.

Word Limit

A constraint placed on the length of the AI-generated response. Word limits help control the depth and brevity of the output and are commonly used for tasks like summarizing or creating concise content.

Zero-Shot Learning

A method where an AI model generates responses to prompts it has never seen before, based on its general understanding of language and the task at hand. Copilot leverages zero-shot learning to respond to a wide variety of user inputs without needing retraining for each task.

This glossary provides a foundational understanding of key concepts when working with Microsoft Copilot and prompt engineering. Whether you're just starting to explore Copilot or you're looking to deepen your expertise, this terminology will help you better navigate the world of AI-assisted productivity and refine your prompts for optimal results.

www.ingramcontent.com/pod-product-compliance
Lightning Source LLC
Chambersburg PA
CBHW080555060326
40689CB00021B/4861